ED
.05

ED

)

:D

Also published by Mowbray by David Hay

Exploring Inner Space

Religious Experience Today

Studying the Facts

David Hay

MOWBRAY

Mowbray
A Cassell imprint
Villiers House, 41/47 Strand, London WC2N 5JE, England

First published 1990

British Library Cataloguing in Publication Data

Hay, David, *1935–*
    Religious experience today: studying the facts
    1. Religious experiences
    I. Title
    291.42

ISBN 0-264-67072-8

Typeset by Colset Private Limited, Singapore
Printed and bound in Great Britain by
Biddles Ltd, Guildford and King's Lynn

Contents

For Jane

Preface

Over the past twenty years there has been a quiet revolution in our knowledge of the nature and frequency of report of religious or transcendent experience in contemporary Western society. We now have fairly convincing evidence that it is widespread and that, in a word, it is normal. This book attempts to explain how the revolution came about and the part played in it by the Alister Hardy Research Centre (AHRC) at Manchester College, Oxford. I also make claims about the importance of the research findings for modern religion. As a Christian I have in mind the churches, but I believe the facts are of more general importance to religiously oriented people of any persuasion.

From the perspective of the religious believer the findings of recent research are extraordinarily encouraging. We now know with a fair degree of certainty that, for a majority of people in Western society, religious interpretations of reality are not mere abstractions, but are rooted in personal experience. Unfortunately, this religious 'empiricism' tends to be damaged, even crushed, by a catastrophic loss of morale because of a widespread taboo concerning religion, arising from Enlightenment ways of thinking. More specifically, traditional scientific interpretations of the world make religion an embarrassment for many who are unaware of modern developments in science.

Paradoxically, the recent increase in our knowledge of religious experience has come about primarily through the curiosity and the research of people working in universities and trained in the natural and social sciences. At the end of the nineteenth century, science and religion were supposed to be at loggerheads, but we have come a long way since 1901, when Andrew White published his celebrated *History of the Warfare of Science with Theology in Christendom*. It is now apparent that the methodology and perspectives of empirical science arose within the presuppositions of the Christian religious tradition and that the relationship between the two is complex and intertwined.

More than that, the critiques of religion that so powerfully hold the field today arose not simply from reflection on the findings of empirical science, but also from certain philosophical presuppositions that have influenced both the direction and the interpretation of scientific research in a way that has narrowed it and, at times, dehumanized it. Mercifully, it is coming to be recognized that science is a human enterprise conducted by people with minds, emotions and, dare I say it, an holistic or religious dimension to their apprehension of the world.

Modern research is showing us that it is a mistake to think that the realm of human experience I am choosing to define as 'religious' is something remote, esoteric, or the preserve of an aristocracy of spiritual adepts. Even at the turn of the century, William James was claiming that religious awareness is part of human nature, universally present as a potential in every member of the species.

This biological view was taken up enthusiastically and made more explicit by Professor Sir Alister Hardy, zoologist and founder of the Centre in Oxford which bears his name. From 1974 onwards I had the privilege of working for the Centre, and from 1985 to 1989 was its director. In that role my task was to ensure that the policy of ontological neutrality with regard to the reality of religious experience was adhered to. Having now concluded my term as director, I feel more able to express my views as a committed member of a religious community.

At the time of writing, the Centre, under its new director, Dr Gordon Wakefield, is about to move its headquarters from Manchester College to Westminster College, Oxford. Manchester College has a link with the study of religious experience going back to the end of the nineteenth century, and played host to the Centre from the moment of its foundation in 1969. It is therefore appropriate to thank the College and its officers for their important part in the growth of this research tradition.

On behalf of the AHRC, it is important also to acknowledge the financial support that has enabled the work of the Centre to continue and expand. In a society that, at least publicly, has other things on its mind, it takes courage to give backing to a research programme which strays across the frontiers of science and religion. I want to acknowledge in particular the help of the Templeton Foundation, the Dulverton Trust, the Fairbairn Trust, the Hibbert Trust, and the Moorgate Trust, as well as the continuing financial support of over 600 members of the Centre.

I have benefited from the wisdom and advice of many friends and colleagues in the development of my reflections on these matters. My debt in the first place is to the chairman of the Alister Hardy Research Centre, Lord Bullock, for his unwavering personal support and trust in my judgement. Secondly, I am deeply grateful to Bishop George

Appleton for encouraging me in my belief, in the face of criticism from certain quarters, that this research has importance for the churches. I also want to thank colleagues, past and present, here and in the United States, whose ideas and support I have been especially aware of during the writing of this book: Geoffrey Ahern, John Franklin, George Gallup, Arthur Gray, Andy Greeley, John Hickey, Mike Jackson, Oliver Knowles, David Lewis, Bill McCready, Meg Maxwell, Ann Morisy, Edward Robinson and Polly Wheway. Finally, I am grateful to May Orton for word-processing the initial text of this book, so that I could edit it to my heart's content.

David Hay
February 1990

1
Religious experience and science

Unitarians in Oxford

Holywell Street in Oxford nestles close to the heart of the university. Behind its pleasant but not particularly distinguished houses lie, on one side, Hertford College, and on the other, Wadham. As the street approaches the junction with Mansfield Road it is bounded on its right-hand side by the great sandstone bulk of New College. Opposite New College and with its main entrance on Mansfield Road is Manchester College, blending naturally and elegantly with the surrounding university buildings, though it is in fact an independent, Unitarian foundation.

Its origins can be traced back to the rise of the eighteenth-century dissenting academies in the north of England, in particular Warrington Academy, which had among its distinguished associates John Dalton, who propounded the atomic theory, and Joseph Priestley, who discovered oxygen. The tradition of 'devout religion and indefatigable scientific zeal', characteristic of Unitarianism, was brought to Oxford in 1889 when the decision was made to set up Manchester College in the centre of the English religious and academic establishment.

The vice-principal of the new college was Joseph Estlin Carpenter, son of the distinguished physiologist W. B. Carpenter, who had been professor in the Royal Institution in London. With regard to religion, Estlin was brought up in stormy times, when the duel between traditional religion and science was at its most fierce, centred as it was on Darwin's theory of evolution. There is no evidence that Carpenter was disturbed in his twin allegiance; to him as a Unitarian, evolution was simply the mechanism of a more profound Divine creation.

However, the young Carpenter did not entirely escape the experience of his religion becoming dry and barren. The importance for the story I am unfolding is that his relief (which came in 1864, the same year as T. H. Huxley and Bishop Wilberforce's notorious tussle over evolution at the British Association's meeting in Oxford) was via a religious experience. The account of it, which is contained in a letter to a friend, is worth quoting in full; it describes a type of perception, as he interpreted it, which was to become the subject of scientific investigation over 100 years later in Manchester College.

I was in a condition of religious apathy for a long time when I was at Manchester New College [then in London]. I had no intellectual doubts: I do not think I am able to enter into them: that means perhaps that I had not widely departed from the philosophy in which I was trained. But though I had no doubts, I had no religion. I had no sense of personal relationship to God. I thought that I ought to leave the College for services were a weariness to me. I never wished particularly to pray. I hoped that if I went for a time to work in some way among the poor and the ignorant, my religion might in some way be renewed in me. It was brought about not in that way. Dr. Martineau persuaded me to wait in the College, and one summer I went to stay with Wickstead at his father's house in North Wales. Shall I tell you what happened to me? Well, I shall not see you smile, and I have no secrets from you. You know how to respect confidences. I went out one afternoon for a walk alone. I was in the empty unthinking state in which one saunters along country lanes, simply yielding oneself to the casual sights around which give a town bred lad with country yearnings such intense delight. Suddenly I became conscious of the presence of someone else. I cannot describe it, but I felt that I had as direct a perception of the being of God all round about me as I have of you when we are together. It was no longer a matter of inference, it was an immediate act of spiritual (or whatever adjective you like to employ) apprehension. It came unsought, absolutely unexpectedly. I remember the wonderful transfiguration of the far off woods and hills as they seemed to blend in the infinite being with which I was thus brought into relation. This experience did not last long. But it sufficed to change all my feeling. I had not found God because I had never looked for him. But he had found me; he had, I could not but believe, made himself personally known to me. I had not gone in search of a satisfying emotion, I did not work myself up into this state by any artificial means. But I felt that God had come to me, I could now not only believe in him with my mind, but love him with my heart. I cannot tell you how often this has come back to me, both with thankfulness and with humiliation. . . . I am often perplexed to know why such revealings do not come to other souls. But I cannot regard this as a mere piece of romanticism, though I shall not be surprised or offended if you do. This event has never happened to me again . . . it was not necessary. The sense of a direct relation to God then generated in my soul has become a part of my habitual thought and feeling.[1]

01 Carpenter believed that this experience was the enduring foundation of his religious life and, no doubt combined with a natural tranquillity of temperament, it gave him an unshakeable confidence in the reality of that dimension of life. Because of the seemingly fundamental quality of his experience, it also led him to become curious about the universality of religion.

Soon after he arrived in Oxford, he became friends with two of the founding fathers of the study of comparative religion, Friedrich Max-Müller, whose rooms were a few hundred yards away in All Souls College, and E. B. Tylor, the director of the Oxford Museum. Carpenter himself was to make important contributions in this field.

Estlin Carpenter and religious experience

Where it is possible to examine the private lives of those who have made a major contribution to study in this field, almost without exception the initial stimulus is to be found in a vivid experience of transcendence. I am personally convinced that it was this fleeting moment of Estlin Carpenter's life experience that gripped him and gave him the conviction that religion is something found universally in people. The encounter had come upon him so unexpectedly and suddenly, yet with such power, that unless he was to dismiss it as a temporary mental aberration, he had to regard it as a true revelation of the nature of reality.

In 1894 Carpenter went to the United States, as a visiting special preacher at Harvard University. While there, he met Edwin Starbuck, who was a pupil of the first professor of psychology at Harvard, William James, the brother of the novelist Henry James. Starbuck played a very important part in the founding of the scientific study of religious experience. He was the first person to construct a questionnaire that inquired about people's experience of religious conversion.[2] At that time, 'conversion' was probably still the most striking phenomenon of the religious culture of Protestant America. Especially in the case of New England, its religious origins in Puritan and Pietist faith were possibly more dominant than in any other comparable sphere of European religious influence. The avowed intent of the founding fathers had been to make it so, far away from contrary and persecuting religious currents in Europe. Starbuck was ideally placed to make his study of conversion.

His research must have struck a chord with Carpenter, because when he returned to Manchester College he took with him some questionnaires for distribution among the staff and students. As far as I am aware, these were the only copies of Starbuck's questionnaires distributed beyond the confines of the east coast of North America. So in a rather uncanny way, Manchester College played a part in the very beginnings of the scientific study of religious experience.

Within a few years, William James himself crossed the Atlantic to give the Gifford Lectures of 1901 and 1902 at Edinburgh University, published as *The Varieties of Religious Experience*[3] and significantly subtitled 'A study in human nature'. James drew heavily on examples of contemporary experiences of conversion provided by Starbuck. The lectures were wildly successful, and within six years James was again in Britain, this time at the invitation of Carpenter, to give the Hibbert Lectures in the library of Manchester College. They were so well attended that the library became overcrowded and they had to be shifted to larger premises in the Oxford Exam Schools.

Carpenter himself cannot be reckoned a member of the small group of major figures in the foundation of the study of comparative religion, but he was a not inconsiderable contributor. As I have noted, he was in touch with a number of the major scholars in the English-speaking world who were concerned with it. I think we can see in him the expression, via a Unitarian background, of the classical religious preoccupations of the educated Victorian. That is to say, he was fascinated by the potentially painful boundary between science and religion.

In 1913 he published a small book entitled *Comparative Religion*,[4] and in dipping into it one can see the perspectives that are of interest to him. Carpenter's axiom was that religion is something deeply built into all of us; in other words, it is in fact primeval or even primitive. For him, religion was 'One phase of human culture; it expresses man's attitude to the powers around him and the events of life. Its various forms repose upon the unity of the race.' Furthermore, 'the old classifications based on the idea that religions consisted of a body of doctrines which must be true or false, reached by natural reflection or imparted by supernatural revelation, disappeared before a wider view. Theologies may be many, but religion is one.'

Carpenter's views coincided with those of many of his scientific contemporaries, in that he interpreted the whole history of religion as being established on the basis of evolution. Although there might be instances of decline in religious practice, the general movement was from crude and less complex forms, towards refined and developed ones. Therefore, he felt that if one wanted to get at the roots of religion, one should look at it in its primary forms among so-called primitive peoples, or in the 'animism' exhibited by young children.

Thus, he was interested in the case of a small child who, impressed by the power and speed of a tramcar as it thundered along its track, offered it a bun; perhaps, thought Carpenter, we can see here the roots of religious sacrifice or propitiatory prayer. The third chapter of *Comparative Religion*, 'Religion in the Lower Culture', investigates the appearance of the sacred in primal culture as expressed by terms like *mana*, *wakanda*, *orenda*, *mulungu*, etc. Anthropologists of this period were very interested in these manifestations, and one senses in Carpenter's short chapter a parallel fascination that may not be unrelated to a curiosity about his own experience of the sacred in his twentieth year.

Carpenter assumed religion to have emerged during the last period of the Great Ice Age, and had in mind the conjectural evidence that can be adduced from Neolithic cave paintings and burial rituals. Carpenter felt that to understand the meaning of these symbolic remains, there must be a return to the internal world of thought and feeling, an opinion not too remote from that of modern phenomenologists of religion. He noted that the study of the origin of religion had been adverted to by the German theologian Friedrich Schleiermacher (another and more eminent forerunner of modern phenomenology) at the beginning of the nineteenth century, with his suggestion that religion begins with the 'feeling of absolute dependence'.

Nowadays, said Carpenter, the study of religious origins has passed out of the hands of philosophers and theologians and into the hands of psychologists, who are the scholars best equipped to study the nature of wonder, awe and reverence. Because of the universality of religion, no single religion can be selected as a standard for the whole human race. It is necessary to examine all the data, or as many of the data as possible. When one is confronted by the variations in religion, however large, one is looking at the effects of climate, of food supply, of geographical distance and the like. An analogy can be made with geology, which explains the many forms of the land by a set of general theories; or ethnology, which explains the variations between peoples. However, underlying all these varieties is the same reality.

Looking for origins

Estlin Carpenter's own faith may have been untroubled, but the questions in which he was interested haunted our Victorian and Edwardian forebears. During the nineteenth and early twentieth centuries, a suspicion about religion that had been growing steadily since the European Renaissance finally turned, for many, into a full-blooded rejection.

It is important to realize that this rejection was a European rejection, not to be found in non-European cultures. It arose out of the experience of people who, whatever their geographical location, lived their lives in the context of a history and set of beliefs originating in the continent of Europe.

Rejection of religion spawned a new academic industry, answering the questions that came in its wake. For those who had decided that religion was a human invention, the next question to be answered was 'When?' And along with that were other questions concerning 'How?' and 'Why?' Much of the most interesting research and speculation of nineteenth- and early twentieth-century scholars (for example, Auguste Comte, Ludwig Feuerbach, Herbert Spencer, J.G. Frazer, Sigmund Freud, and Carpenter's friends Max-Müller and Edward Tylor) concerned these problems.

The question 'When?' meant looking for traces of religion in the life of the species *Homo sapiens* when it was first emerging; or perhaps looking at the relics of even more ancient primates, the Neanderthal people. But searching backwards into prehistoric times for the beginnings of a phenomenon that we see around us today is always a hazardous occupation. And more so in the case of religion. However one tries to think of it, religion seems to imply something intangible, and that is precisely what is entirely inaccessible when one searches the relics of the remote past. In a pre-literate culture, all that archaeologists are able to unearth are the physical objects that human beings leave behind.

Estlin Carpenter equivocated. He stated that it was a waste of time looking for origins, but also that he could not help being fascinated by the question. In spite of his doubts, and perhaps because of a parallel curiosity, archaeologists have sometimes thought it plausible to put a religious interpretation even on very ancient remains.

One such example is located in the Palaeolithic period, a time even more remote than the point Carpenter had speculated might be the moment when religion had first evolved. In 1939, quarrying operations on Monte Circeo on the Italian coast, halfway between Rome and Naples, uncovered the entrance to a cave which had been sealed up by a landslide for tens of thousands of years. When A.C. Blanc, the man who first reported on the contents of the cave,[5] entered it for the first time, he found there was a low chamber at the rear which could only be entered on hands and knees. Inside, lying on a mound of earth and stone, was a human skull surrounded by a circle of stones. Originally, the skull had probably been set up on a stick which had since rotted away. The strangeness and the eeriness of the discovery, which must have affected Blanc very powerfully, made him wonder whether what he had discovered was the tangible remains of a very ancient magico-religious cult.

But when academics argue about these matters, they find it impossible to come to any firm conclusions. How could they? The frustration one has in trying to imagine the inner life of people so remote from us, is because we cannot reach the workings of their minds. All that can be done, once as much evidence as possible has been gathered, is to make an educated guess that probably includes (if one is honest) an effort at empathizing with the inner experience of the cave dwellers.

Many scholars would condemn these attempts at empathy as extremely naïve. But equally, one is at liberty to question such scepticism. Prehistoric cave dwellers, like present-day members of primal cultures, did not have access to the vast body of information available to the computer-literate inhabitants of the Western world. But if these cave dwellers survived into adulthood, they had the same amount of time to acquire human wisdom, as opposed to technical information, as today's inhabitants of New York or London or Oxford.

It is possible to overdo the pessimism about reaching imaginatively into the remote past. One is very well aware today of the great power of social structure and relationships in moulding our consciousness. It is therefore rather easy to downplay the fact that the other major realities that feed our creativity are exactly the same as those that played upon the thoughts of prehistoric people.

Biologists tend to be optimistic in this respect. Members of the same, or closely related, species living on the same planet share a considerable amount of common ground, in that their anatomy and physiology are similar, their perceptual apparatus is similar, they share the experience of being born, living in communities, eating, breathing, excreting, growing, reproducing, suffering physical and mental disease, growing old, witnessing the death of others, and anticipating their own death. Only if one believes that the world of the mind is something totally separated from direct bodily experience, can one suppose that the consciousness of our remote ancestors was utterly different from our own.

A universal phenomenon?

Estlin Carpenter and a number of his contemporaries suspected that religious experience and belief are permanent elements in the life of the human species, because they appeared to be present in all cultures studied by nineteenth-century anthropologists. The issue is not straightforward, however, not least because there is no universally agreed definition for religion. Perhaps the most that can be said is that 'religious people' who come from Western cultures seem to recognize and be recognized by 'religious people' from other cultures.

The difficulty is to determine what it is that is mutually recognizable. If it is claimed to lie in a common striving after God, it can be rightly objected that some of the great world religions, Buddhism for example, do not necessarily include a belief in God. This fact has led some scholars to say that Buddhism (at least in its Southern form) is not really a religion, but instead a philosophy of life.

In fact, Christianity and Buddhism provide a striking and paradoxical example of intellectual contrast combined with parallel practice. Christianity and Hinayana or Southern Buddhism are historically about as distant, both geographically and ideologically, as it is possible for two great cultural systems to be, and yet still lay claim to a common ascription as 'religions'. Yet, at the level of practice, the common ground is unmistakable. Religious adepts in both systems, when they undertake their most characteristic discipline, that of meditation or contemplation, have the following requirements:

The requirement to be silent.

The requirement to be still.

The requirement to be aware or receptive.

The requirement to lead a celibate life, at least for a time.

The requirement to follow the rule of a spiritual director or meditation master.

The requirement to abide by the ethical norms of one's culture.

On reflection, it is surely amazing that overlaps of this kind are found in cultures that have grown up over thousands of years, completely independent of one another. However, the similarities become a little less extraordinary when account is taken of the common biological heritage mentioned earlier.

Ignorant as they were of scientific methodology or sophisticated data collection, our primeval ancestors nevertheless had the same curiosity as their present-day descendants about all that they experienced. Without such curiosity, they, like us, would be unable to adapt to their environment and survive. Among the rest of the incoming data, and in no way separated off from it, one may speculate that there were intimations of what we would now label the realm of the transcendent. Investigating this in the same way as any other part of life, discoveries would have been made by trial and error which led to the growth of a relatively coherent body of knowledge about it.

Physical and mental stilling increases one's ability to be aware in all dimensions of experience,[6] perhaps including the transcendent. The requirement for sexual abstinence may have something to do with the necessity to discard the notion of the desiring self (or even, in the Buddhist case, denying its reality). The necessity to learn from a director may be because what is being assimilated is a set of very subtle technical skills and therefore the novice is in the same role as a craft apprentice. It is also understandable why there is an ethical requirement; the modern growth of understanding of mind/body interactions makes it predictable that the mental peace that results from behaving ethically also has a physiological effect.

There is now very strong evidence that meditation or contemplation has measurable biochemical and physiological effects on the body. It is known, from comparative measurements made on Christian and Buddhist monks[7] during meditation, that they enter a very similar physiological state and, in particular, the brain rhythms recorded by both appear to be identical. Furthermore, when the conversation between Eastern and Western meditators turns to their spiritual paths, although at the conceptual level they appear to be at loggerheads, there is a striking claim of common insight when it comes to the practicalities of the experience.

Whether such similarities are true of all religions remains very uncertain. Nevertheless, it does appear to be true that most, if not all (including so-called primal religions), imply a practical investigation of kinds of experience which appear to transcend normal everyday life, via prayer, meditation, trance or other altered states of consciousness.

Religious experience as a Protestant discovery

What I have been implying above is that the religious quest is a very ancient and universal aspect of being human, and that it is not inappropriate to label our species, as some have done, *Homo religiosus*. I have been at pains to make clear my view that it is a biologically natural phenomenon, but now I wish to return to the other side of the coin, the social.

The vast variety of religions can be accounted for in the same way as modern linguists sometimes account for the multitude of languages. Religious 'competence', one might conjecture, is built in or structured into us in a way analogous to linguistic competence; the vast and colourful differences are the result of the human skill of varying whatever can be culturally varied.

If human beings belong to a religion which, as in Christianity, has a doctrine of Grace, it would be more acceptable or appropriate to speak of the desire for God leading people to learn to wait, or to seek ways of opening themselves to Divine influence. But in every religion, the traditional search has operated within the context of a personal religious commitment; it has not been something about which people have been able to feel detached, as if they were looking at religion from the outside.

Nevertheless, it was within European Christian culture that it first seemed reasonable to undertake a careful investigation of religion from the position of a disinterested observer. Partly, this is to do with the appearance of widespread scepticism about religion throughout the eighteenth century. Subscribers to this viewpoint, who felt that they had emancipated themselves from religion, were left with the need to find an explanation for the stubborn errors of religious people. Partly, because culturally mediated forces affect all who participate in the culture, educated believers became 'divided selves' in religious matters, with a consequent pressure to investigate their religion in a new, more detached way.

The conceptualization of 'religious experience' as something clearly separate from the rest of life only began to be tenable when religious interpretations of reality started to decline in power, and it became possible to imagine a range of human experience that was *not* religious. Of course, mystical experience was known about long before the advent of Christianity, and within Christianity long before the Reformation. But it was not for many years afterwards that the category of 'religious experience' appeared, and even then only in Protestant circles. In the English language, for example, the first printed reference to religious experience was not until 1809.

Associated with this, there are two remarkable facts about the history of attempts to make a scientific study of religious experience. First, they were initiated almost exclusively in the New England states of America towards the end of the last century. That is how Estlin Carpenter came across the idea. Secondly, like Carpenter, the great majority of students of religious experience up to and including the present day, came from a Protestant Non-conformist background. From what I have been implying earlier, there is no reason to suppose that the realm to which religious experience refers is the exclusive territory of Protestant Christians; indeed, I have just been suggesting that it may be universal. So what led to the curious phenomenon that I have indicated?

It seems to have stemmed from the aftermath of the Reformation and is connected with an interest in the process of religious conversion that arose in the sixteenth and seventeenth century among English Puritans and German Pietists. What concerned both was the psychological experience of being 'saved'. 'Born again' Christians can trace the popularity of that famous phrase within Evangelical circles to the influence of the eighteenth-century Pietist leader, Auguste Herman Francke.[8] Pietism and Puritanism met and powerfully influenced the consciousness of New England, especially in the eighteenth century when Methodism arrived to add its own enthusiasm to that of the Puritan settlers.

The religious energy of New England at that time was most vividly represented in the genius of Jonathan Edwards. His popular fame rests on his hellfire preaching, but his importance more justly rests on his ability as a philosopher and as the founding father of the psychology of religion.

Edwards's sermons on hell are masterpieces of a grim art. They were used by him in an attempt to bring people to a state of terror about the fate of their eternal souls, and thus to the point of repentance and, by the Grace of God, conversion. It was a system that appeared to work. But it would be a mistake to think that Edwards confined his understanding of religious experience to conversion.

In 1746 he published *A Treatise Concerning the Religious Affections*,[9] which is about discernment, how to recognize genuine Christian experience. While he recognized the importance of the moment of conversion, Edwards quite clearly believed that religious experience involves much more than that. Perseverance in devout faith almost required that there should be a continuation of perceptible communication with God, and he maintained that there was a special sense in the devout person, the 'sense of the heart'.

Edwards must have been convinced by experimental evidence for this in his own life, since he regularly reported times in which he was aware of, or had 'views' of, Christ. In addition, he gave lyrical descriptions of an altered awareness of nature, almost Wordsworthian in mood:

> The appearance of everything was altered; there seemed to be as it were, a calm, sweet, cast, or appearance of Divine glory, in almost everything. God's excellency, His wisdom, His purity and love seemed to appear in everything; in the sun, moon and stars, in the clouds and blue sky; in the grass, flowers, trees; in the water and all nature; which used greatly to fix my mind.

The power of religious experience in the social life of New England probably also had to do with the fact of its isolation from the sceptical temper in eighteenth-century Europe. But by the nineteenth century, improved communications were bringing the isolation to an end. At that point the breadth of the category of religious experience was greatly increased, through the efforts of the New England Transcendentalists, of whom the leading figure was Ralph Waldo Emerson. The son of a Congregational minister, he himself was in the Unitarian ministry for a time, but was not impressed by the cold rationalism which by that time had replaced the rich feeling of Edwards's faith.

Emerson's response was to broaden the search for transcendence. Edwards, had he foreseen such a turn of events, could only have been aghast, for the Transcendentalists dispensed with the exclusiveness of

Christianity and either played down or abandoned any notion of Grace.

Emerson was not unlike Edwards, an inheritor of the New England religious temperament, but a man whose faith in historical Christianity had been destroyed by modern rationalism. His solution was to replace it with a romantic mysticism which incorporated elements of Asian religious philosophy. Having despaired of reason and in any case not having Edwards's philosophical brilliance, Emerson's system depended primarily not on rationality, but on insight; or, as he liked to describe it, Reason, which sees to the heart of things and can be considered the equivalent of intuition. Here, I can perhaps recall Estlin Carpenter's debt to intuition for the power and stability of his own religious convictions.

William James and the New England School

The person who tied the New England religious tradition together with modern empirical science was William James. His father, Henry James senior, had in his youth attended Princeton Theological Seminary, intending to become a Presbyterian minister. He found the seminary not religious enough, left it and, though he came to reject Calvinism, remained a deeply devout man all his life. His friendship with Emerson, combined with his own leanings, no doubt had a strong effect on his son William, though he was to resist his father in religious matters. William was also a true modern, with a scientific and cosmopolitan education. His language when he writes of religion is that of empirical science. It is not really surprising that Carpenter, with his somewhat similar background, should find the New England students of religious experience to his taste.

The friendly link between psychology and religion that was strengthened by James was also maintained by a number of other American scholars in New England. It even led to the brief existence of something called the Emmanuel movement in Boston, which was an attempt to develop a religious version of psychotherapy. But there were already some New England psychologists who were not so sympathetic, most notably James Leuba, who was Swiss by origin, and thus perhaps rather more strongly in touch with European scepticism than his American colleagues. His personal prejudice was to explain so-called religious experience as misinterpretation of some other phenomenon, probably sexual in nature.[10]

Professor G. Stanley Hall also recognized the link between religion and sexuality, though he was much more ambivalent than Leuba in his interpretation of the implications.[11] Along with William James he was a founder of the new science, yet it was he more than anyone else who was to sow the seeds which virtually destroyed it. Hall was president of Clark University in Massachusetts and founding editor in 1887 of the *American Journal of Psychology*. He was also an enthusiastic admirer of Sigmund Freud, who at that time was beginning to be recognized as a figure of some eminence on the other side of the Atlantic. In 1909, to celebrate the twentieth anniversary of the founding of Clark University, Hall invited Freud, Jung and other leading European psychoanalysts to visit the United States. William James, near the end of his life and in failing health, attended the celebrations at Clark and was impressed by Freud, though angered by the latter's dismissal of the Emmanuel movement as dangerous amateurism.

The Clark University meetings had a much greater impact in the United States than Hall could have anticipated. As founder of the nation's premier psychological journal, he assisted the process. An examination of the issues of the *American Journal of Psychology* published in the aftermath of Freud's visit reveals how powerfully the new discipline affected American thought. A surge of articles on psychoanalysis appeared. From the religious perspective, they added considerable weight to the argument that sought a pathological origin for religious belief and experience.

Ironically, Americans had already been prepared by James for an interpretation of religious experience which relied on a realm beyond normal consciousness. What Freud added was the idea of repression: that material that arose into consciousness, apparently from somewhere else as is the case with religious experience, represented in disguised form the contents of the unconscious mind. In Freud's opinion, the material that was repressed into the unconscious consisted of socially unacceptable sexual and aggressive desires (perhaps especially in a Puritanical community such as New England then was). Religion thus operated as a socially acceptable outlet for the neurotic fantasies resulting from repression.

There seemed to be a correlation with Stanley Hall's hitherto rather confused reflections on the links between sexuality and religion, and also the assertions of Leuba. Freud's ideas focused what had up to that time been a blurred explanation, especially to a generation becoming more sceptical about religious matters, and therefore looking for other ways of explaining them.

Something else was happening in America. A new homegrown branch of psychology was about to appear on the scene led by someone else in revolt against his strict Evangelical upbringing. In 1913, John B. Watson, the founder of the discipline of psychology called behaviourism, put another nail in the coffin of the psychology of religion. Watson was contemptuous of the kind of psychology he saw around him; in his view, his colleagues were wasting time with unmeasurable intangibles, the supposed contents of consciousness. Examination of subjectivities of this kind, thought Watson, could never lead to any dependable objective knowledge. The only observable and measurable dimension of psychology was behaviour.

As I have repeatedly asserted in this chapter, religious experience is intangible and certainly not measurable in a way that Watson would have approved of. So his claim that the domain of consciousness was not a proper sphere for psychological investigation immediately put out of court attempts to study the consciousness of the presence of God.

The result of the combined influence of psychoanalysis and behaviourism was to produce a severe split between those who saw themselves as academic psychologists investigating the mechanisms operating in religious experience, and committed religious believers primarily concerned to protect their beliefs. Inevitably, the briefly flowering new academic discipline went into decline and virtually disappeared by 1930. For most practical purposes, it had resolved itself into a study of psychopathology on one side and religious faith on the other.

On the other side of the Atlantic in Manchester College, similar forces were no doubt conspiring to diminish the influence of Estlin Carpenter's parallel point of view. Carpenter has been called a God-intoxicated man who was also profoundly convinced of the importance of the scientific method. He died in 1927 and perhaps was a sad witness of the tearing apart of the two realms that concerned him.

Estlin Carpenter's notion of religion was that it is 'one thing', though theologies may be many; that it is something natural to the human species. His powerful statement on behalf of his belief was that 'Unitarianism is not a denial of any dogma, but an assertion of dogmatic freedom by the vindication of religion as greater than dogma'. From a contemporary perspective, his claim may seem naïve. The singularity and incredible variety among the religions of the world may suggest that it is a mistake to try to disengage them from the culture, the creeds, the local and temporal circumstances of their origins. Nevertheless, in Manchester College, some 40 years after Carpenter's death, a new lease of life was given to an old idea.

Notes

1 Quoted in C. H. Herford (ed.), *Joseph Estlin Carpenter: A Memorial Volume* (Oxford: Clarendon Press, 1929).

2 E. D. Starbuck, *The Psychology of Religion* (New York: Walter Scott, 1899).

3 Two currently available editions are those by Fontana (1960) and Penguin American Library (1982).

4 *Comparative Religion* (Home University Library, 1913).

5 Described in Johannes Maringer, *The Gods of Prehistoric Man* (London: Weidenfeld & Nicolson, 1960).

6 See, for example, M. West, 'Meditation', *British Journal of Psychiatry*, vol. 135 (1979), p. 457.

7 Reported in William Johnston, *Silent Music* (London: Fontana, 1976).

8 See P. C. Erb (ed.), *Pietists: Selected Writings* (London: SPCK, 1983).

9 Reprinted in paperback by the Banner of Truth Trust (Edinburgh, 1986).

10 See James Leuba, *The Psychology of Religious Mysticism* (London: Kegan Paul, Trench, Trubner & Co., 1925).

11 *The Psychology of Adolescence* (2 vols; New York and London: D. Appleton & Co., 1904).

2

A scientist's vow

Alister Hardy

In 1896, only a few years after Manchester College had moved to Oxford, Alister Hardy, who was to have so much influence in reawakening the tradition begun by Estlin Carpenter, was born in Nottingham. Hardy was the third son of a well-to-do Nottingham architect, and from a very early age he became passionately interested in natural history. At the age of fourteen, he was sent to public school at Oundle, then under the headship of Sanderson, its most famous master. Sanderson was a leading light in the introduction of science education into public schools in that period, and Hardy quickly became involved in the study of biology.

Oundle is set, even now, in a beautiful rural part of Northamptonshire and Hardy's interest in natural history was given full rein. A defect in one of his eyes meant that he had a lifelong problem with stereoscopic vision. He was therefore unable to participate in the extensive sports activities so beloved of English public schools. While others were on the playing fields, he spent many hours by himself, wandering through the countryside. Reading his autobiography, it is clear that these lonely walks had a large influence on what was to follow.

There was a little lane leading off the Northampton road to Park Wood as it was called, and it was a haven for the different kinds of brown butterflies. I had never seen so many all together. The common Meadow Browns, of course, were everywhere in the fields but here also were the Lesser Meadow Brown or Gatekeeper, the Wall Brown and Marbled White, which belongs to the same family. As one approached the wood, there was a small covered reservoir with grass banks leading over it and this was always the home of many Ringlet butterflies, of which I seem to remember there were two forms recognised as a variety. I specially liked walking along the banks of various streams watching, as the summer developed, the sequence of wild flowers growing along their brims. I was attracted by several streams lying in different directions from Oundle. I wandered along all their banks, at times almost with a feeling of ecstasy.[1]

It is apparent from his writing that Hardy was discovering the nature mystic in himself. He described how, during these walks, he felt the presence of something that was beyond and yet, in a way, part of all the things that thrilled him—the wild flowers, and even the insects too. It was at the age of 88 that he noted down something that he had never told anyone before:

> Just occasionally when I was sure no-one could see me, I became so overcome with the glory of the natural scene that for a moment or two I fell on my knees in prayer—not prayer asking for anything, but thanking God, who felt very real to me, for the glories of his kingdom and for allowing me to feel them. It was always by the running waterside that I did this, perhaps in front of a great foam of Meadow Sweet or a mass of Purple Loosestrife.

On the academic side, it became clearer and clearer to his biology teacher that his interest in nature, especially insects, must be leading him towards a career in biology. It was decided to send him to Oxford to take a diploma in forestry so that he could specialize in the study of forest insects. Hardy was well aware of the enthusiasms of the great Victorian naturalists, particularly Darwin and Wallace, and in fantasy thought of himself as emulating their exploits. In October 1914, with hansom cabs still to be seen on the streets of Oxford, he took up residence in Exeter College, a few hundred yards from Manchester College, where Estlin Carpenter was still the principal.

Making a vow

The strains in a culture are felt to a greater or lesser degree by all its members, and Hardy was no exception. Although he started off in forestry, he was in fact already deeply interested in the more profound issues of biological theory, particularly the Darwinian interpretation of evolution; he therefore decided to switch to zoology.

In the zoology department he found a gulf between his own mystical intuitions and the mechanistic, and perhaps implicitly anti-religious, interpretations of evolutionary theory that were expounded. He was studying in the very university where, in 1860, the most notorious argument in modern scientific history took place between T. H. Huxley and Samuel Wilberforce, then Bishop of

Oxford. It is part of the folklore of science that at a public meeting held under the auspices of the British Association for the Advancement of Science, the two men were invited to debate the validity of Darwin's theory. Wilberforce was there to demolish it but, according to some of the more prominent verbatim reports, it was Wilberforce who was made to look both unprincipled and an idiot.

Present at the meeting, and no doubt applauding Huxley, was John William Draper, an American who in 1874 brought out a book which, in its day, was extremely successful—*A History of the Warfare Between Science and Religion*.[2] As the title indicates, he depicted the advance of empirical science as a military triumph for the forces of enlightenment over religion's legions of darkness. Today, such a picture looks excessively simplistic, but there is still enough of the mood of those days around to give one a whiff of the venom in the air.

By a curious coincidence, Hardy himself was tutored by Julian Huxley, grandson of the great T. H. And so it was at Oxford, in what feels like another era from our own, that Hardy became convinced of the importance of bringing about a reconciliation between evolutionary theory and the spiritual awareness of humanity. It was also at that time that he made a vow. This was not, he says, a prayer, but—aware that he was about to take part in the First World War—he made a promise ('to what I called God') that if he should survive it, he would devote his life to attempting to bring about a reconciliation that would satisfy the intellectual world.

The realities of war meant that he had to leave Oxford in the same year that he arrived, to join the army with a commission as a second lieutenant in the First Northern Cyclist battalion. Even there, he continued to feel that, in a strange way, his fate was being controlled. In his autobiography, he quoted from a description someone sent during the 1970s to the Religious Experience Research Unit, which Hardy eventually set up in Manchester College. The reason he included it was that it closely resembled his own experience:

> When I was about sixteen, or perhaps a little earlier, I began to have what I call 'a sense of destiny'. It was only long afterwards that I realised that Napoleon and Hitler were the supreme examples of 'men of destiny' and that no good came of it. Though it explains nothing, I consoled myself with the thought that this was an example of the polarities of life. This sense of destiny is still with me—I suppose some people would call it 'guidance', but that implies a personal 'guide', which is no part of the experience.

It so happened, and perhaps Hardy would have seen this as destiny, that he had a relatively quiet war. He returned to Oxford in 1919 to take up his course in zoology. In his class there were only three students, one of whom, Sylvia Garstang, was to become his wife.

He had not forgotten his vow, but the excitement of his studies, and the need to forge a career, meant that for a time it had to fade into the background. His future father-in-law Professor Walter Garstang, while not dissuading him from keeping to his long-term plan, warned him of the importance of making his name in the field of orthodox science before he began to embark on rather more dangerous, or even eccentric, territory. Dutifully, and no doubt wisely, that is what he did.

For a time he worked as a naturalist in the Fisheries Department of the Ministry of Agriculture and Fisheries, before becoming chief zoologist to the *Discovery* expedition to the Antarctic in 1924–28. On his return he was appointed, at the age of 32, to the chair of zoology and oceanography at the University of Hull. In 1942 he became regius professor of natural history at the University of Aberdeen, and in 1946 he was given the Linacre Chair of Zoology at Oxford University, which he occupied with the highest distinction until 1961, extending his career in Oxford for a further two years as professor of zoological field studies.

Hardy was known to generations of zoologists as one of the world's foremost marine biologists and a great teacher and advocate of Darwinism. Innumerable young biologists learnt their evolutionary theory from the book that he edited in 1954 with his Oxford colleagues, Julian Huxley and E. B. Ford, *Evolution as a Process*. He was an Oxford DSc, a Fellow of the Royal Society and the Zoological Society. In 1939 he received the scientific medal of the Zoological Society for his work on marine and aerial plankton. In 1957 he was knighted for his work in marine biology. In 1968 he received in Washington the Phi Beta Kappa award for outstanding contributions by scientists to the literature of science, for his book *Great Waters*.

Keeping the vow

Sir Alister had fulfilled the ambitions of his father-in-law and reached the top of his chosen scientific profession, but over the years his ardent interest in the possibility of a 'biology of the spirit' had not abated. As far back as 1925, when he was working in the Antarctic, he had already asked a press agency to collect newspaper cuttings concerning religion.

He had been thinking how it might be possible to collect random samples of religious experience from the general public. Those were the days before public opinion polls. The incident that sparked off his decision to survey the press occurred just before he set off for the Antarctic. He saw an article in a newspaper describing how a medical

officer in the Royal Air Force had been awarded a prize for his
research. The officer remarked that he wished to acknowledge that he
could never have done the work had he not received help through
personal prayer.

It occurred to Hardy that perhaps many such incidents might be
recorded in newspapers and then forgotten. So before he sailed, he
wrote as follows from the RRS *Discovery* to the General Press Cutting
Association in London:

Dear Sirs,

I should be glad if you would collect for me, until further notice,
from the newspapers mentioned below all the cuttings—news or
articles—dealing with or referring even remotely to:

Religion
God
Faith
Prayer
Relations or antagonism of Religion and Science.
Anything in fact of a religious or spiritual nature,

provided that they are not
Ecclesiastical or church notices or news, reports of services or
sermons (*unless* arousing public interest or controversy), obituary or
other notes on the lives of ministers of any denomination, or
dealing with psychic research, spiritualism and kindred subjects
(*unless* in a religious connection).

I enclose a cheque for £5.5.0 in payment of the first thousand,
and wish you to begin at once. I am likely to be away for close on
two years on the Discovery Expedition, and instead of sending me
the cuttings I should be glad if you would keep them for me, unless
I give other instructions, in envelopes, separating them
chronologically into months.

In reading such a letter, I am reminded of the model of the Victorian
collector, whose apprenticeship (as in the case of Darwin and Huxley)
included a lengthy biological expedition to remote corners of the
earth, and the writing of courteous requests to gather information
about different species. In this case, the examples being sought were
sub-species of *Experientia religiosa*. It looked as if they were beginning to
emerge from their obscurity. While in the Antarctic he heard that the
press agency had collected 1,000 cuttings, and by the time he got back
to England there were 2,000 waiting for him.

Hardy then had to take up his new post as professor of zoology at

Hull and thus became immersed in creating the department; therefore, it was quite impossible to deal with the cuttings. However, he could see that they were unlikely to give him sufficient examples of the kind of religious experience he was looking for, although they did reflect the general feeling of the populace at that time in relation to spiritual matters.

He was able to repeat the same operation in 1935–37 and again in 1945–46. This last collection was, he found, most disappointing. He had to employ a different press-cutting agency; so whether it was a result of the change in methods of collection, or because of a greatly reduced public interest in matters of religion, he did not know. But both the number and the quality of the cuttings were much poorer than those of his earlier samples. It must have seemed like the end of a promising idea.

Expanding the idea

Then in 1948, when he was already professor of zoology at Oxford, Hardy gave a lecture in the Priestley Hall in Leeds. It was in this famous centre of Unitarianism, where 180 years ago the scientist Joseph Priestley had lived and worked, that Hardy again publicly made his views clear:

> Anyone who thinks at all about other than trivial everyday things, must strive to arrive at a viewpoint from which all aspects of experience appear to be consistent with one another. Such a viewpoint is our philosophy. We must be unsettled and uncomfortable if we cannot arrive at such a harmony of experience. I am sure that today so many are intellectually bewildered. Science has made such progress that they have come to have a real faith in it. Then, when they hear some of the more vocal of our leading biologists proclaiming a mechanistic—a materialistic—interpretation of life, they find their faith in science in conflict with an intuition which speaks to them of spiritual reality. One or other must be an illusion. Which is it? I am sure that the answer to that question is far more important to mankind than the discovery of atomic power.[3]

There is no doubt whatsoever that the former question was by far the more important for Hardy himself.

It was in 1951, in the course of an Essex Hall lecture entitled 'Science and the Quest for God',[4] that he made his first suggestion for the setting up of a special institute to make a systematic study of religious experience. The urgency of the proposal, as Hardy saw it, lay in a perception that, as Lord Elton had said, 'we are for the present living on our spiritual capital'. When he retired from the professorship of zoology at Oxford, Hardy was given the opportunity to express his views more fully. He was invited to give two series of Gifford Lectures at the University of Aberdeen. In the second series, entitled *The Divine Flame: An Essay Towards a Natural History of Religion*,[5] given in the natural history department in Marischal College, Aberdeen, he expressed his faith.

The Gifford Lectures

Hardy's starting point could be taken from a remark made by Aldous Huxley, the brother of his old tutor at Oxford: 'Much of the restlessness and uncertainty so characteristic of our time, is probably due to the chronic sense of unappeased desires from which men naturally religious, but condemned by circumstances to have no religion, are bound to suffer'. It was this obstinate conviction that religion is something natural to us—and that, for many people, has been made difficult or impossible by a mistaken intellectual tradition—that drove Hardy to speak out. His theme was that a scientific theology, or a natural theology to use Lord Gifford's phrase, could encourage research and collect facts systematically to show the scientific world that there is overwhelming evidence that religious experience has been, and is still, an important aspect of human behaviour. In other words, that there are patterns in religious experience and that ordinary people, through the help they receive from this area of their experience, are able to accomplish things that they would normally consider beyond their capacity. Hardy thought that if such a scientific theology were to come about—and he did not believe that it would happen for another century—the bringing together of a vast natural history of religious experience would demonstrate that what was being examined was in fact real.

There is a major distinction between the new approach advocated by Hardy and the old-style natural theology that was in vogue in the nineteenth century, and best represented by Archdeacon Paley's *Natural Theology*.[6] Typically in the latter, an attempt was made to demonstrate the inevitable conclusion that there must be a God because of the order to be found in nature. Paley tried to show that the extraordinary adaptations of animals and plants to their environment must indicate the existence of a Divine Maker, in the same way that the design evident in a watch indicates an earthly watchmaker. Darwin thought Paley's *Natural Theology* was the only worthwhile textbook he read while a theology undergraduate at Cambridge. Nevertheless, his explanation of the origin of species by the power of natural selection seemed to dispose of that particular method of deducing the reality of God. Before the end of the nineteenth century Paley was no longer thought important enough to be on the required reading list for theology students at Cambridge.

Hardy's idea was much more direct. What he wanted to do was to build up a natural history of the human experience of the 'sacred' or 'divine'. From the point of view of evolutionary biology, it seems very clear that we have evolved to 'fit' the world. During the course of evolution those genetic variations that increase the likelihood of an individual surviving in its environment have, so to speak, been selected by nature. It is because they are better adapted to the environment than other individuals that they are less likely to perish. So, for example, if an individual's sensory apparatus and awareness fit it better for its environment than other members of its species, it is more likely to succeed, to survive, to reproduce and so to perpetuate its genes. What then of 'religious awareness'? Has that evolved because it fits us for the world? Hardy certainly believed it to be the case.

He turned in particular to the work of social anthropologists to try to demonstrate that some awareness of the sacred is more or less universal in the human species. His starting point is the French sociologist Emile Durkheim, who, in his book *The Elementary Forms of the Religious Life*,[7] made a study of the religion and religious experience of Australian aborigines. Durkheim was aware of the special quality of religious experience. Although his understanding of Australian religion is considered out-of-date by most modern anthropologists, his feeling for the experiential centre-piece is surely recognizable to the religious believer, and therefore, from that perspective, is not entirely misconceived:

> Totemism is the religion, not of such and such animals or men or images, but of an anonymous and impersonal force, found in each of these beings, but not to be confounded with any of them. No one possesses it entirely and all participate in it. It is so completely independent of the particular subjects in whom it incarnates itself, that it precedes them and survives them. Individuals die, generations pass and are replaced by others; but this force always remains actual, living and the same.

Elsewhere Durkheim emphasizes just how very different from other kinds of experience religious experience is:

> . . . generally the disputes, of which religion is the theme, turn about the question whether it can conciliate itself with science or not; that is to say whether or not there is a place beside our

scientific knowledge for another form of thought which would be specifically religious.

But the believers, the men who lead the religious life and have a direct sensation of what it really is, object to this way of regarding it, saying that it does not correspond to their daily experience. In fact, they feel that the real function of religion is not to make us think, to enrich our knowledge, nor to add to the conceptions, which we owe to science, others of another origin and another character, but rather, it is to make us act, to aid us to live. The believer, who has communicated with his God, is not merely a man who sees new truths of which the unbeliever is ignorant; he is a man who is stronger.

Sometimes Durkheim's interpretation of religious experience as the 'effervescence' that occurs in certain crowded religious gatherings, particularly among Australian aborigines, is taken to be a dismissal. Hardy felt otherwise. He believed that Durkheim was pointing beyond a simple restatement of historical materialism. As Durkheim says in *The Elementary Forms*:

> That would be misunderstanding our thought to an extreme degree. Ensuring that religion is something essentially social, we do not mean to say that it confines itself to translating into another language, the material forms of society and its immediate vital necessities . . . but collective consciousness is something more than a mere epiphenomenon of its morphological basis, just as individual consciousness is something more than a simple efflorescence of the nervous system.

Quoting from other anthropological studies, Hardy pointed out that the same kind of experience seems to be referred to in many cultures, and here there is an echo of the views of Estlin Carpenter. Thus, among North American Indians, tribes belonging to the Sioux family speak of 'a pre-eminent power to which all the others have the relation of derived forms and which is called *wakan*'. *Wakan* 'embraces all mystery, all secret power, all divinity'. In another part of the world, the Melanesian islands of the Pacific, what appears to be the same force is found under the name of *mana*. Durkheim believed that it was the exact equivalent of the *wakan* of the Sioux.

Hardy referred to numerous other Victorian, Edwardian and more modern anthropologists to try to demonstrate just how widespread the idea of the holy or the sacred is in human society. He felt that it is very closely and directly connected with the same experience among Europeans. On this point he is in agreement with one of the greatest European students of the sacred, the German philosopher-theologian

Rudolph Otto. It was Otto who, in the earlier part of this century, coined the term 'numinous' to describe the special quality of religious experience. He most certainly held the view that numinous experience was a universal, extending even to versions of religion that appear, on the face of it, to be 'atheist'. Thus, at one point in his most famous book, *The Idea of the Holy*,[8] he wrote:

> I recall vividly a conversation I had with a Buddhist monk. He had been putting before me methodically and pertinaciously the arguments for the Buddhist 'theology of negation', the doctrine of *anatman* and 'entire emptiness'. When he had made an end, I asked him, what then nirvana itself is; and after a long pause, came at last the single answer, low and restrained: 'bliss—unspeakable'.

Going back into written European history as far as one cares to go, there is evidence of the same kind of experience. It appears with full force, for example, in the mystical writing of Plato and, following him, the neo-Platonists. Nearer our own times, we see perhaps the same sentiment as found in the Australian aborigine or the Sioux warrior, or the Sudanese tribesman, appearing in the sophisticated Victorian man of letters, John Ruskin. Writing about nature in *Modern Painters*,[9] he said:

> . . . although there was no definite religious sentiment mingled with it, there was a continual perception of Sanctity in the whole of nature, from the slightest thing to the vastest; an instinctive awe, mixed with delight; an indefinable thrill, such as we sometimes imagine to indicate the presence of a disembodied spirit. I could only feel this perfectly when I was alone; and then it would often make me shiver from head to foot with the joy and fear of it, when after being some time away from hills, I first got to the shore of a mountain river, where the brown water circled among the pebbles, or when I first saw the swell of distant land against the sunset, or the first low broken wall, covered with mountain moss. I cannot in the least describe the feeling; but I do not think this is my fault, nor that of the English language, for I am afraid no feeling is describable.

Similarly, Richard Jefferies, nineteenth-century nature mystic and far from any religious orthodoxy, wrote in his extraordinary book *The Story of My Heart*:[10]

> I was not more than eighteen when an inner and esoteric meaning began to come to me from all the visible universe, and indefinable aspirations filled me. I found them in the grass fields, under the

trees, on the hilltops, at sunrise, and in the night. There was a deeper meaning everywhere. The sun burned with it, the broad front of the morning beamed with it; a deep feeling entered me while gazing at the sky in the azure noon, and in the starlit evening.

In selecting these passages, Hardy was insisting that the 'sacred' (the word 'God' may or may not be the correct one) is constantly bursting out beyond orthodoxy, beyond the churches. He was struggling to set the human sense of the sacred free from the constraints of a religious orthodoxy which, at times—but, I want to insist, not always—is little different from secularism in its attempt to set boundaries to what we are permitted to experience as real.

The word 'religion' itself is a difficult one which upsets many people, but which still retains a powerful positive connotation for others. Hardy quoted with approval the anthropologist Malinowski, who said of religion that it 'makes man do the biggest things he is capable of'. For Hardy, the feeling of being in touch with a reality beyond the self is as much something biologically real as, for example, the experience of being in love. Religious experience is not something recordable by physiological measurements, any more than love is. But, like love, it is manifested in us as embodied living creatures and will have physiological events associated with it. In that sense, we could expect that it would be present, to some degree, in all living creatures. Hardy commented: 'It would not surprise me, could we know it, if this experience of an emotional contact with something greater than the self, which we are only just beginning to express with difficulty in words, would seem to be a development of some animal feeling of joy . . .'. For this reason, Hardy called for the building up of a great natural history of religious experience from many different fields: biology, anthropology, sociology, psychology, and psychical research. A famous previous Gifford lecturer at Aberdeen University had been the theologian Karl Barth, who disconcerted the sponsors by spending his lectures explaining why a natural theology was invalid, on the grounds that it is a misconceived attempt to constrain God within human parameters. In a counter-attempt to disarm critics of a Barthian complexion, Hardy used an analogy. The relation between natural theology and God, he says, is rather like the relationship between the science of optics and the experience of light. The overwhelming reality of our direct experience, which so far transcends us as individuals, does not mean that the investigation of our response to it is not worth while. In the same way, what we are exploring in the kind of natural theology that Hardy envisaged is the nature of the human response to the transcendent.

The Religious Experience Research Unit

It was a strange twist of fate, or serendipity, that in 1966, at the same time that he was waiting for the galley proofs of his Gifford Lectures to be delivered, Hardy decided to try to set up the Religious Experience Research Unit in Manchester College. I know from personal conversation that he was quite unaware of the direct link with the work of William James and E. D. Starbuck in the United States at the turn of the century. In his initial proposal to the Council of Manchester College, he noted:[11]

> Just as Nuffield College is a centre for research in social studies, I would like to see Manchester College, in addition to being a teaching institution, become a recognised centre for research into those fields which are fundamental to what a modern liberal religion is all about: religious experience, the nature of man's personality and his relation to divinity.

Hardy had in mind some examples of the kind of studies that he would like to see undertaken:

> 1 An extension and development of those pioneer studies by Professor E. D. Starbuck (*The Psychology of Religion: An Empirical Study of the Growth of Religious Consciousness*, 1899) and by William James (*The Varieties of Religious Experience: A Study in Human Nature*, 1902). These classics have never been added to in the same spirit in which they were undertaken; and they were confined to studies of people (mainly university students) of a particular Protestant Christian community. As James says regarding Starbuck's work, 'the enquiry ought to be extended to other lands and to populations of other faiths'.

> 2 Surveys and analyses by questionnaire of other mystical experiences among different populations—on the lines of the agnostic author Marghanita Laski, in her *Ecstasy: A Study of Some Secular and Religious Experiences* (1961).

The idea was to make a start in a very modest way, using one room in the tower of the College. Eventually, after a number of vicissitudes, the Unit was opened in September 1969 at 24 Holywell Street which, up to that time, had been a shop. At the age of 73, and with very little money indeed, Hardy had launched the Centre into existence.

Notes

1 This and certain other quotations presented in Chapter 2 are drawn, with permission, from the unpublished typescript of Hardy's autobiography.

2 Published in New York.

3 *The Faith of a Scientist* (London: Lindsey Press, 1948).

4 (London: Lindsey Press, 1951).

5 (Collins, 1966); reissued by the Religious Experience Research Unit, Manchester College, Oxford (1978).

6 *Natural Theology; or, Evidences of the Existence and Attributes of the Deity collected from the Appearances of Nature* (London, 1802).

7 English translation by J. W. Swain (London: Allen & Unwin, 1915).

8 English translation by J. W. Harvey (Oxford University Press, 1950).

9 John Ruskin, *Modern Painters*, vol. 3 (London: George Allen).

10 (London: Eyre & Spottiswoode, 1949).

11 From a memorandum submitted to the Council of Manchester College in 1966.

3
Natural religious experience

How do you start?

In a sense, the whole structure of modern biology was built on the vast collections of specimens made by Victorian naturalists on their field trips, at first near to home, but then to remote parts of the world. The task that the Religious Experience Research Unit set for itself during the early years of its existence was the building up of an analogous collection of accounts of religious experience, beginning with the local environment: Britain.

At first, Hardy sought the help of the editors of what in retrospect seems a relatively limited range of newspapers and journals, since they all had a Christian interest. They extended from the *Catholic Herald* at one end, through all different kinds of Protestantism to Unitarianism at the other end of the spectrum. He wrote articles for them, appealing for help with the collection of material and, because religious experience is so difficult to define clearly, gave some examples to illustrate what he meant.

His first example was taken from Beatrice Webb who, with her husband Sidney, founded the Fabian Society. She had expressed her practical philosophy of life by saying that 'for my own part I find it best to live as if the soul of man were in communion with a super-human force which makes for righteousness'. This religious feeling was sometimes induced by the appreciation of great music or by corporate worship. But it also led her to achieve a religious interpretation of the whole of reality, which meant that she was upheld and able to seek guidance in prayer without compromising her intellectual integrity.

Hardy's second example was taken from the successor to Estlin Carpenter as principal of Manchester College, L.P. Jacks. In his Hibbert Lecture of 1922, Jacks had stated:

All religious testimony, so far as I can interpret its meaning, converges towards a single point, namely this. There is that in the world, call it what you will, which responds to the confidence of those who trust it, declaring itself to them as a fellow worker in the pursuit of the Eternal Values, meeting their loyalty to it with reciprocal loyalty to them, and coming in at critical moments when the need of its sympathy is greatest; the conclusion being that wherever there is a soul in darkness, obstruction or misery, there also is a Power which can help, deliver, illuminate and gladden that soul.

As his third example, Hardy took a quotation from the anthropologist R. R. Marett. Marett, like Hardy, believed that the characteristic manisfestation of religious consciousness was recognizable at all times and in all places.

It is the common experience of man that he can draw on a power that makes for, and in its most typical form wills, righteousness, the sole condition being that a certain fear, a certain shyness and humility, accompany the efforts so to do. That such a universal belief exists amongst all mankind, and that it is no less universally helpful in the highest degree, is the abiding impression left on my mind by the study of religion in its historic–scientific aspect.

The choice of examples is significant. All three of the people Hardy had selected were highly intelligent and independently minded. One was the founder of a radical political movement, another was a leading member of a religious body that strongly dissents from traditional Christian orthodoxy, and the third was an eminent anthropologist. In addition all spoke of a power that has both a supportive and a moral effect on the life of the individual.

Hardy was suggesting to his readers that the stereotype of 'religiosity' as something adhered to only by submissive and not very intelligent people need not necessarily be true. The intuition that directed Hardy's choice was important. As we shall see in a later chapter, fear of the stereotype of the religious person is one of the most potent forces in leading people to remain silent about their spirituality.

Readers of the articles were asked to consider whether they had ever been conscious of, and perhaps influenced by, a power, whether they called it the power of God or not; this power might either appear to be beyond their individual selves, or in part outside and in part within their being. If such was the case, they were invited to write to Professor Hardy, describing their experience and its effects on them. He also asked for details of their age, sex, nationality, religious upbringing, and any other factors that might be relevant.

The first response was depressing. Having had a piece accepted by some 30 journals and expecting several thousand accounts, Hardy was very disappointed when he received barely 200 replies. Further-more, they were very unrepresentative of the total age range of the population or its gender balance; a high percentage of the responses were from elderly ladies. The fact that many of them were obviously very intelligent and articulate did not help to assuage the feeling that the Unit was, after all, chasing after examples of experience that were well on the way to becoming extinct.

It was not until the decision was made to shift attention to secular newspapers that the fortunes of the Unit changed. Articles appeared in the *Guardian*, the *Observer* and *The Times* and, along with an appeal made through the BBC, and some other minor articles in the United States, Australia and New Zealand, Hardy accumulated another 1,500 accounts. This time they covered a wider age range and were somewhat more balanced in relation to gender; strangely, it seemed that by looking first in the religious press he had begun his search in the wrong place.

Starting to classify accounts

Having accumulated a reasonable number of specimens, the next step for the natural historian is to start to produce a classification or taxonomy. Trying to classify written accounts proved to be a much more complicated business than attempting to classify specimens of animals or plants. To begin with, there was an extraordinary range of variation in written expression; some people wrote an account on the back of a postcard, others sent in pages and pages of single-spaced typescript. Obviously, the content had been heavily influenced by factors like facility with language, cultural background and personal belief, and this immediately posed problems.

On a first examination of the collection, what seemed to be possible was to split the accounts of experience into two types: what might be called the 'numinous' experiences, that is, broadly speaking, experiences of the presence of God, and, in contrast, more 'mystical' experiences, where the writer is talking about something like a 'merging' with the rest of reality. In fact this kind of classification fits well with the categories suggested by a number of philosophers of religion. But it was soon to become clear that the taxonomy would have to be much more complex than that.

There was also the question of the quality of the records. Hardy was quick to admit that there were some descriptions which, as far as he could see, fell neither into the numinous nor the mystical category, but into a third category he labelled Z. They included those that came from what is unkindly called the 'lunatic fringe'; some were actually sent from psychiatric hospitals. Another popular stereotype therefore looked uncomfortably as if it had a grain of truth in it. Nevertheless, writings coming from unbalanced people were very much less frequent than he had expected; furthermore, they were all carefully filed, because it was by no means certain that they did not contain elements worth studying—at the very least, perhaps providing material for use by psychiatrists.

Then there was the question of honesty. With regard to the main body of accounts there was, of course, no way of being certain about the integrity of those who had written in. No doubt some descriptions were exaggerated, perhaps to feed the self-importance of the writer, but Hardy felt that no one with an unbiased mind could read the majority without being impressed by a sense of their deep sincerity. Having read a large number of them myself, I agree.

Very early on, it became clear that quite a number of the writers had never spoken to anyone else about their experiences, even though they might relate to events of very great personal significance, such as tragic bereavements or broken lives. It began to be feasible to believe that a phenomenon was being uncovered that had hitherto been an almost totally hidden universe of human experience, at least in contemporary society. Hardy likened it to the experience of the early marine biologists: 'We are at present like the first collectors of marine plankton, dipping our little nets into the sea from a rowing boat and marvelling at the variety of life brought forth, just as the marine naturalists were doing a hundred years ago'.[1]

Religious experience and childhood

Having accumulated a considerable number of records and attempted to catalogue them in some way, the next step was to look at the pattern of relationship they had to people's lives. Appropriately, one of the earliest major studies examined the first occurrence of a religious experience.

In his pioneering research into conversion experiences in New England, Edwin Starbuck had discovered that the commonest time of life for a conversion to be reported was in adolescence. It was as if religious experience only became possible when people had achieved a certain level of maturity. Perhaps, as some modern theorists of the subject would say, you cannot have a religious experience without the right kind of cultural background or language—almost as if you have to be educated into it. One of the most attractive studies done on the materials collected by Hardy was an examination of the religious experience of childhood,[2] and I believe this casts doubt on this 'social construction of religious experience' thesis.

Edward Robinson, who joined the Religious Experience Research Unit very early in its existence and was later to become its director, was fascinated by one of the features of the material collected. Although no request had been made to informants to state the earliest point at which experience occurred, a total of 15 per cent of the correspondents went back to experiences that occurred in their earliest years. Robinson was very struck by the frequency of remarks like, 'the most profound experience of my life came to me when I was very young, between four and five years old'.

As an educationalist, Robinson found himself reflecting on the theories of the development of thinking processes in children which are widely taught in departments and colleges of education. Probably the most famous of all students of cognitive development is the Swiss psychologist Jean Piaget. Although in some respects psychology has moved on since Piaget's day, his attitude is very typical of many contemporary child psychologists. The most basic intellectual fact about children, as far as these psychologists are concerned, is an absence of ability. Children do not have the capacity to understand the world in the way that adults do, and the task of the student of cognitive development is to determine the sequence of developmental stages the child goes through to achieve intellectual maturity. Another way of putting this might be to say that adulthood liberates us from the illusions that we have when we are children.

In the realm of religious education, this assumption led one well-known student of this field, Ronald Goldman,[3] to conclude that religious insight does not begin to appear until the age of twelve or thirteen. Robinson's study of the records made him doubt very much if this is true. He began to feel that the experiences of childhood, what Edwin Muir has called the 'original vision', are actually a profound form of knowledge; perhaps knowledge that we can lose or forget as we grow older. These experiences are very similar in character to mystical experiences reported in adult life; they may be identical, and they have a quality that is self-authenticating.

By 'self-authenticating' Robinson meant two things. First, religious or mystical experiences have authority. Their immediacy and power is itself a guarantor of their truth. One of his correspondents said, 'if it was a hallucination, why do I remember it as the most real and living experience I have ever had? It was like contacting a live wire when you were groping for a match.' The other way that these experiences are self-authenticating is that they seem to bring to the person who has them an awareness of his or her true self, underlying the self-deluding subterfuges that so often appear to be necessary for survival in a threatening world. This is partly a discovering of one's uniqueness, but also a revealing of one's value; that one has, so to speak, as of right, a place in the whole of reality. The following example, given by Robinson, describes this sense of being 'placed in the universe' very well:

The first approach to a spiritual experience which I can remember must have taken place when I was five or six years old at the house where I was born and brought up. It was a calm, limpid summer morning and the early mists still lay in wispy wreaths among the valleys. The dew on the grass seemed to sparkle like iridescent jewels in the sunlight, and the shadows of the houses and trees seemed friendly and protective. In the heart of the child that I was, there suddenly seemed to well up a deep and overwhelming sense of gratitude, a sense of unending peace and security which seemed to be part of the beauty of the morning, the love and protective and living presence which included all that I had ever loved and yet was something much more.

The writer is trying to convey the ecstasy of the experience and does so successfully and movingly because of competence in the use of language. But we can perhaps be misled, as Robinson says, into the habit of thinking of 'mystics' as though they were some different kind of human being with a special sensitivity that the rest of us lack. Perhaps also, we tend to think that special 'triggers' such as the beauties of nature are necessary for this kind of experience to occur. The person who wrote the above has a facility with language and refers vividly to the beauty of nature as the context of the experience. In a later part of the book I will look at the question of triggers, so I will simply register at this point a question mark over the necessity for them.

I am also doubtful whether 'mystics' are unusual in that they are confined to those who know how to write or speak articulately. The fact that someone is inarticulate does not mean that they do not experience life with vividness. On the contrary, sometimes a sophisticated use of language can even give a false sense of meaningfulness. All the evidence from the thousands of attempts at description in the files in Oxford supports the traditional view that religious experience is well-nigh inexpressible, probably because it escapes or transcends the influences of everyday cultural construction. While adults may have the education and the articulation to convey meanings, their intoxication with words, at the expense of direct experience, may mean they are prone to distort the communication of its inner nature.[4] As Robinson says, religious experience is not the same thing as pious uplift or emotional self-indulgence or, I would add, beautiful rhetoric; it is much more like a direct confrontation with reality.

The other side of the coin is of course that we need language and an interpretation to mediate our experience, and these are derived from our life history. Robinson refers to someone who became a writer, first on Marxism and then on theosophy, who writes to the Unit of his experience as one of being conscious of vague mysterious laws that challenged his understanding. Someone else talked about her mystical experience in 'organic or structural terms'. Thus she 'understood that this was the living tissue of life itself in which that which we call consciousness was embedded'. This person was an art teacher who was a specialist in architecture. Yet a third description, coming from someone who is a management consultant and an adviser on industrial relations, speaks of 'love' and 'friendliness' and of 'a protective and living presence'.

We would need to know much more about the life stories of these and other individuals to be quite sure of the connections. Nevertheless, they do suggest that upbringing and temperament are what provide people with the medium through which experience comes. For that reason we might guess that the beauties of nature are not so much a 'trigger' for religious experience, as the realm in which it is acceptable for it to occur, simply because of our knowledge of the poetry of nature mystics like Wordsworth. The inexpressible is inexpressible because language talks about bits of experience—not the whole of our experience. Perhaps the special faculty of childhood is to have a holistic simplicity. Thus, one of Robinson's informants says, 'I suggest that this was able to happen because I was still whole with the simple wholeness of childhood, before my being was broken up into pieces at school'.

The loss of the 'whole' is not the only factor that places such experience under threat. Also, where teachers cannot believe in the reality of the experience in pupils, naturally enough the censorship of the prevailing culture means that it will very often be lost or repressed. There may be a serious flaw in contemporary religious education, which tends to favour a very objective stance towards religion and teaches children a great deal about the external facts. Nevertheless, because it fails to make a coherent examination of personal experience, in practice most children have only fragments of their own inner experience to hang on to, without the apparatus of language and interpretation that a culture provides. Again, this is something I will return to in later chapters.

Not that religious experience or feeling can be defined purely in relation to the language and rhetoric of religious organizations. Robinson remarks cynically that we might as well try to discover about sporting spirit by looking at contemporary organized sport. So it may often happen that people whose natural religious awareness is very rich, are turned away or repelled by what they find in the institution: 'Churches seemed peopled by the listless, the fanatical or the ostentatious. Nobody seemed to mean what they said or sang; they went because they Ought To; or out of a superstitious fear or unease, or for sentimental reasons. There was nothing wonderful.'

Nevertheless, the institution does provide a language which, while it may not mean very much at the time that it is first assimilated, can later become of great importance. The reason for this is the way that experience of this kind, though it may take only a fraction of a second, remains as something potentially important throughout the life of an individual. For example, the following quotation is illustrative:

> One might say that recollection of it acts as a kind of tap root to springs of life. It became very active, this early experience, very active in my mind some five years ago when I suffered a very great bereavement, the greatest I suppose that a man can have. And then this original experience was called upon by some part of my personality; it asserted itself and became very active. There was a strength there, a strength or comfort. It was an assurance, a guarantee that I know.

Robinson ends his book, which I recommend as a refreshing antidote to much of the colourless literature in the field of religious education, with the following remark:

> One might say then, in justification of such a study as this, to have attempted an assessment of the childhood experience of any of these writers at an earlier age would have been in some respects at least premature; that they would not yet have had their experience, or not yet had it sufficiently for a proper judgement to be made of it. A remarkable instance of this slow process comes from a man who had never been able to forget a vaguely mystical experience he had had more than fifty years before. At the time and for long after, it had little effect on him: 'I was the same man after as before'. Reflecting on its subsequent influence he is only sure of one thing: it had not had the effect it might have if he had made more of it. He goes on:
>
> > The remarkable thing as I now see about such seeds, stored as bare memories of experiences which in the past have fallen on unreceptive ground, is their capacity to remain dormant for long periods, perhaps waiting inertly for an auspicious change in the soil which contains them.
>
> Later in his letter the writer actually thanks us for having brought him to reflect on this long buried experience, and so having enabled it to germinate.

A speculation about childhood

The notion of recovering what has been lost by the conscious mind, as a major educational task, has some very eminent precedents in the world of education, notably Plato. It is from him that we received a model of the teacher that is still too radical for many people. A teacher, says Plato, is not someone who knows, passing on knowledge to someone else who does not know. Teachers who are true to their task actually do something very different; they attempt to recreate the subject in the minds of their pupils by getting them to bring to conscious and articulate awareness what they already know, but have forgotten or perhaps repressed.

Let us suppose for the moment that Robinson is right, and that in many cases adults have forgotten or repressed the transcendent experience of childhood. In such a case, much of what goes on in religious education today can only be seen as misguided and misguiding.

The notions of Ronald Goldman or, more recently, James Fowler[5] in the United States, suggest a concentration on cognitive development as of great importance in religious education. I do not wish to dispute that assertion in itself; obviously, children should be helped to achieve maturity in thinking about religion, and in this respect Goldman and Fowler have much to teach us. But simply to concentrate on this aspect may be to skate over and avoid the heart of the matter. Perhaps what we should be doing is helping with the recovery of the holistic vision of early childhood that has become obscured by analytical thinking or, to use the current jargon, the dominance of the left-hand side of the brain.

Seen from this perspective, most of the practical activities of religious people can be seen as attempts to recover the larger, intuitive vision. In the first place, prayer and meditation can be understood as ways of waking up from the fragmenting illusions engendered by the surrounding barrage of messages that pour in from our environment. Notice that I am *not* claiming that prayer is world-denying, or some sort of escape from the world. On the contrary, it is through the recovery of the innocent eye that one is able to dispel one's ignorance of the rich reality that surrounds us. At the simplest and most obvious level, people writing to the Oxford Centre regularly describe the increased vividness of their sensory experience of the world when they have engaged in the practice of prayer or meditation.

Another example of the role of religious practice in waking people up is when the reading of sacred scripture is properly understood. Thus, in Christianity, believers do not merely interpret what they read in the Bible as a record of what God said in the past; it can also be experienced by them as what God is saying to them in the here-and-now. This is the basis for an almost universal method of scriptural meditation in which the reader takes a short passage from the Bible and reflects at length on its content. At times this activity appears empty and the reader might as well be gazing at a newspaper, but on other occasions there is the experience of being gripped by the words, which now appear as a direct proclamation by God.

A dramatic illustration of such an experience was portrayed in the film *Chariots of Fire*. The Scottish athlete Eric Liddell, having let down the British team competing in the 1924 Olympics in France by refusing to run on a Sunday, is due on that day to read from the Bible in the Presbyterian church in Paris. Clearly torn, because his mind is constantly flitting away from the service to the international gathering a few miles away, he finds himself reading the sentence 'Before Him, all nations are as dust'. To Liddell, God has spoken, things are in perspective and his mental agony is over.

Religious rituals are another way of reawakening the forgotten sacred. Outsiders often see religious ritual as empty and meaningless; Freud thought it a symptom of neurosis. But the role of ritual in deepening and sensitizing religious awareness makes believers rather dubious of Freud's interpretation. Christianity contains many rituals that enable the believer to relive the central elements of the Christian story. Thus the Mass or Communion Service recreates the scene at the last supper when Christ gave his body and blood to his disciples, in the form of bread and wine.

Again, associated with each of the pivotal moments in life are what anthropologists call 'rites of passage'. In Christianity these rites are linked to a parallel incident in the life of Christ, whether it is the baptism in the Jordan, the wedding at Cana, or Christ's entry into the tomb and subsequent resurrection. Within each of these rites lie a multitude of sub-rituals, including the smallest details of gesture and clothing. The total effect is first of all to remind each believer of the presence of God, and in many cases this is followed by a direct awareness of that presence.

The simple directness of the religious vision is also apparent in the way that devout people often see the whole of life as, so to speak, the language of God. Sometimes this is through the noting of odd or extraordinary patternings of experience, referred to by the psychologist Jung as 'synchronicity'; or people may experience their dreams as religiously meaningful. Most frequently, however, it is the total untidy experience of everyday life that Christians interpret as God's dialogue with them.

This forms the basis for a popular exercise used to help believers to deepen their religious understanding. First, people are invited to write down a list of the images they have of God. Very often a collection of such images will be found to consist of a mixture of metaphors learned in church or school, further tangled up with early memories of parents—what Freud would call a 'projection'. Those who have completed this exercise are then asked to shift from theory to a direct examination of their everyday experience of life during the past few days, and how they have related to God during that time. Frequently there is a startling contrast. Typically, there is a change from a somewhat cold, even threatening, series of abstract images towards something much warmer and more vibrant, perhaps also more challenging. It is here that believers sometimes claim to experience God in the voice of conscience or discontent. In this case their experience is more to them than merely that of making an ethical decision or having a sense of outrage at injustice; it is felt as an encounter, a request from God.

The investigations made by Edward Robinson into the 'original vision' suggest that religious education has seriously fallen short in the task of helping pupils to apprehend this very basic experiential dimension of religion. Many religious education programmes actually work against it, by arranging for religion to be kept as an object for examination at arm's length. To take Robinson's findings seriously would be to revolutionize religious education.

Notes

1   *The Divine Flame* (London: Collins, 1966).
2   Edward Robinson, *The Original Vision* (New York: Seabury Press, 1983).
3   Ronald Goldman, *Religious Thinking from Childhood to Adolescence* (London: Routledge & Kegan Paul, 1964).
4   Concealed behind these remarks is a philosophical dispute about the relationship between language and experience. Aware of the paradox, I am choosing to accept at face value what people have to say about their experience and its relation to language. Temperamentally, I am averse to the hermeneutics of suspicion.
5   James Fowler, *Stages of Faith* (San Francisco: Harper & Row, 1981).

4

The vividness of the Spirit

First attempts at classification

Traditionally, when biologists set about classifying living organisms, they do so by devising a system of relationships that branches and subdivides rather like a tree. Thus we commonly think of two of the major groups into which living things can be divided as plants and animals. The animals in turn can be separated into those with backbones and those without backbones, the latter divisible into fish, amphibians, reptiles, birds, mammals, and so on. The system is meant to be logical, and although in practice it can often be very difficult to use, it means that, in principle, new species can be fitted into it in a way that makes sense. In turning to religious experience, however, the situation is much more complicated because what one is dealing with is not raw experience, but experience expressed in ways that depend on culture, language, personality, life history, gender —all of these factors make the situation extremely complex.

Nevertheless, Hardy's choice of subdivisions, at least in its early stages, was closely linked with biology. To start with, he and his colleague Tim Beardsworth developed a method for classifying the elements into which experiences might be subdivided, according to the five senses.[1] For example, the first element was 'visual experience of a sensory or quasi-sensory nature'. This would include cases where people believed they had had a vision, or perhaps seen a bright light, or felt themselves surrounded by light. A second category was 'auditory'. In this case the person felt that they had heard a voice, perhaps calming or guiding them. A third category was 'touch', and a fourth—in practice a very small group—was where people felt that they had smelt something in a supernatural way. There was no 'taste' category, because no examples were sent in. A final category concerns the 'sixth sense'—supposed extrasensory perception, including such phenomena as telepathy, precognition, clairvoyance, supposed contact with the dead, and apparitions.

Later on, with the aid of Vita Toon, an analysis of the first 3,000 accounts in the files was undertaken and the full classification was published in Hardy's book *The Spiritual Nature of Man*.[2] The full classification tried to take account of behavioural changes; in other words, how the experience had affected an individual's actions. There was also a category for cognitive and affective elements—how the experience was perceived with the intellect and with the feelings. Most common among these responses were: a sense of security, of protection or peace; a sense of joy or happiness; a sense of guidance, vocation or inspiration; a sense of certainty, clarity or enlightenment; a sense of integration, wholeness or fulfilment.

The classification took account of the way an experience had developed some aspect of a person's life, and the period at which the significant development had taken place. In general, these experiences were interpreted as positive and constructive, but a small number were perceived as negative, the latter usually being associated with a sense of the presence of evil.

Among the antecedents, or what I have rather unwillingly called 'triggers' of experience, were natural beauty, participation in religious worship, prayer or meditation, music, literature and drama, depression or despair. Interestingly, the antecedent least commonly mentioned was psychedelic drugs.

Examples of experience

It is impossible in a short book to give a fully nuanced account of these experiences, which are very rich and extremely varied.[3] So what I propose to do is to present some examples of what seem to be the major kinds of experiences that people report.

As hinted when I discussed Edward Robinson's studies, these accounts, when they are torn from the context of a life history and a living individual, often fail to carry the extraordinary force that is transmitted when one is listening directly to someone describing such an episode. This is unfortunate, because I believe it is the intensity, the sense of utter reality and significance that suffuses these experiences, that gives them their power in an individual's life. I have therefore deliberately tried to choose examples from correspondents who are articulate, to demonstrate the mood of the experiences with some degree of sensitivity, in the hope that they will awaken empathy or recognition in the reader.

Synchronicity and patterning of events

This, the commonest of all the categories, normally refers either to an extraordinary coincidence or to a sense that somehow one's life has an unfolding pattern to it. It is often very vague, sensed intuitively, and discovered rather than planned. Thus, it is definitely not the same as the structure one might impose on one's life by, for example, climbing up the promotion ladder in a chosen career.

This group is rather unlike all the other categories, in that the experiences do not necessarily (though they very often will) involve a direct awareness of a sacred or transcendent presence. 'Synchronicity', which I mentioned in a previous chapter, can of course be a matter of trivia. Thus Jung illustrates what is meant by the term[4] by giving the example of a man who happens to notice the serial number on his tramcar ticket. When he arrives home, he gets a telephone call in which the same number is mentioned; and in the evening he buys a theatre ticket, which again has that number. Such an experience may be disconcerting, but it is usually taken to be rather unimportant.

It is when this kind of conjunction happens in association with something that is not trivial, and in a way that assists the individual, that he or she tends to interpret it religiously. My first example comes very close to the one described by Jung—except for the subject matter, which is clearly religious:

> We were watching a play on the T.V. one evening, we did not like it so we switched off and talked. During the conversation, usually nostalgic at our age, I asked the wife if she remembered the words of King George VI . . . at Christmas a while ago about putting your hand in the hand of God; she remembered half of them and repeated them to me. It was nearly 9.00 p.m. and time for the news so we switched the T.V. on again to hear a voice speaking the last line of the play . . . 'Put your hand in the hand of God.' After listening to the news the wife went to get a book and as she opened it a piece of paper fell out containing the complete words . . .

The next example is much more dramatic, relating to the moment when the writer's life was in pieces and she had decided to kill herself:

> . . . at that moment I let out a loud challenge into that dark and lonesome night, into that desolation of land and soul and I shouted: . . . IF THERE IS SUCH A THING AS A GOD THEN SHOW YOURSELF TO ME—NOW . . . and at that very instant there was a loud crack, like a rifle shot [coming from the bedroom]. . . . I stumbled through the open door to my bedroom. I fell into the bed shaking and then something forced my eyes upward to the wall above my bedside table and where I had a very small photograph of my father hanging. . . . The picture had gone—I just looked at the empty space . . . but in looking closer I saw the photograph, face down, on the little table and the narrow silver frame was split apart, the glass broken and from behind the cardboard on the back there

had slipped out . . . the last letter [my father] had written me. . . .
When I picked up that letter and read over and over the words of
this beloved caring father of mine, I knew that was HIS help to me,
and God answered me directly in the hour of this soul being in
anguish.

The recognition of an altogether larger and all-embracing pattern
to life can engender peace even in the midst of considerable suffering.
This is true of the following excerpt, which also illustrates that, rather
than being a symptom of neurosis, religious experience can help
people to come to terms with suffering:

The experiences of the last six months have . . . confirmed my deep
conviction that God is directly and indirectly guiding my life . . . as
well as being absolutely convinced of Divine guidance in the larger
issues of my life, I feel the guidance strongly even in some of the
smaller events . . . the pattern of my life seems to me to be a
mosaic, in which everything, including seeming disasters,
eventually turn to good (e.g. a mental breakdown, frequent eye
trouble, the giving up of my career after thirty years to come home
to look after my parents . . .). I have come to feel almost
apprehensive about the way the rough places in my life have
become smooth . . .

The presence of God

Most typically this is something that appears spontaneously,
sometimes in the most ordinary of circumstances, as in this first
example:

I am surprised that I didn't make a note of the date, but I believe it
happened in spring or early summer of ——. My husband was still
away in the army 'somewhere in England', but in no particular
danger, our son was bouncing about in his pram outside, the sun
was shining and I was making the bed; there was nothing in my life
to make the day different to any other. Suddenly, I was filled with
an absolute certainty of the reality of God. No lights, no voices, no
exotic feelings. Just a quiet utterly convincing certainty 'of course
there is [a] God' . . . it was cool and quiet and certain—and very
surprising.

Another example, from North Wales:

I was a solitary person—not from choice—and I suppose I was
lonely. But in the mountains I felt security and joy and a oneness
with nature. One day, as I stood on a hill above our village, a clear

bright windy day with a breeze rustling the dry heather, it seemed to me that I heard a voice quite distinctly calling me by name. Looking round and seeing no-one I felt suddenly foolish and laughed rather nervously. Then I heard the voice again— '——— —follow me'. That was all . . . no thunder and lightning—simply the wind rustling the heather. I lay down flat on my face and said quite simply 'Lord, I will follow'. As I said, I saw nothing. But a feeling of awe and a presence passing over me caused me to be there for some time, afraid to open my eyes.

Very often the sense of the presence of God is associated with times of fear or anxiety and the experience dissipates the fear. Occasionally there is a visionary element, but in most cases there is no sensory input, even though the presence may be experienced as overwhelming. Here someone describes a moment of panic while in hospital suffering from a severe illness. Although the experience is vivid, there is a slight ambiguity as to whether it was visionary or without sensory input (that is, what St Teresa of Avila defines as an 'intellectual vision'):

. . . the injections were very painful. I dreaded these more than anything. Then the sister came and patted my hand and told me a blood transfusion was to be set up. I fell into a complete, utter and absolute panic. I should scream and no-one screams in hospital— panic mounted. What should I do? I did not think to pray. Then Jesus stood by my ordinary hospital ward bed. It seemed quite natural. He was calm and serene and his whole presence filled me—his calmness and sereneness had a tremendous sense of power and love.

Here is another example illustrating the surprising quality of the experience:

I had an experience seven years ago that changed my whole life. I had lost my husband six months before and my courage at the same time. I felt life would be useless if fear were allowed to govern me. One evening with no preparation, as sudden and dynamic as the Revelation to Saul of Tarsus, I knew that I was in the presence of God, and that he would never leave me nor forsake me and that he loved me with a love beyond imagination—no matter what I did.

My final example of 'spontaneous' religious experience is of great interest because the writer speculates on the use of metaphor:

The experience itself is very difficult to describe. It took me completely by surprise. I was about to start shaving at the time, of all things. I felt that my soul was literally physically shifted—for quite a number of seconds, perhaps 15 to 20—from the dark into the light. I saw my life, suddenly, as forming a pattern and felt that I had, suddenly, become acquainted with myself again after a long absence—that I was, whether I liked it or not, treading a kind of spiritual path, and this fact somehow demanded me to quit academics and enter social work. . . . I must stress here that prior to this experience I used never to use the words such as 'soul' or 'salvation' or any such 'religiously coloured' words. But in order to make even the slightest sense of what happened to me I find it imperative to use them. Looking back it *does* seem as if I saw a kind of light, but I think that this might have been a metaphor I coined immediately after the experience.

Answered prayer

Prayer in times of unhappiness is often an occasion when people become aware of the presence of God. Here is an almost parallel example to the one described above, the one difference being that the woman is actively seeking Divine help:

One evening I wanted to write a letter but was unable to because I was in such a state of grief and misery. I did not know what to do with myself. I had palpitations, breathlessness. I could not stop crying and I was trembling and so restless I had to walk about the room. It must sound extraordinary but I wrung my hands and said aloud: 'I can't go on, what am I to do, I can't bear it!'

Suddenly I realized I wasn't alone and that now I must pray. I said: 'Oh Lord, please help me. I can't go on like this and I don't know what to do.' I stood with my eyes shut. Gradually I was filled with a warm glow inside which increased until I felt I was held in a miraculous light. Time meant nothing, though I do not think it lasted more than half to one minute. Then slowly it left me and when I opened my eyes I was quite calm and composed.

Prayer is sometimes associated with physical healing, as in the case of a woman who had haemophilia:

Two doctors and a specialist —— confirmed that I had this condition, and throughout my childhood the signs continued. Small smooth pink spots appeared round the joints—tiny haemorrhages under the skin—and these were always accompanied by feeling absolutely exhausted. Then followed haemorrhage from the gums so

45

that I woke in the morning with my face and the bedclothes covered with blood. . . . One day, quite suddenly, I said to myself 'Our Lord healed a woman who had haemorrhages—in a way I need the same help. He is still alive. I'll ask to be made well.'—so I said a brief prayer, got up from my knees, said again 'now that will be quite all right'. I have no other explanation of the fact that from that day I became a person of enormous energy—no signs of haemophilia, and the capacity to work and work with the utmost vigour.

But answered prayer need not always be in time of distress. Many accounts come from moments of simple delight. Elderly people, perhaps because they spent their childhood in a more overtly religious culture than ours, often do not appear to need to be as self-consciously religious as is the case in a more secular age. They frequently speak with childlike simplicity of their experience, as in the case of this old sailor, nearly 90 years of age, recalling an incident from his youth:

When I was passing for Seaman Gunner at —— I had the morning watch; it was a lovely summer morning about 5 a.m. I was very happy, enjoying the Lord's presence with me, when I said 'You know Lord, I have never discovered a bird's nest'. A voice seemed to say, 'Walk quietly and you will see one in a few minutes; now lift your foot and press lightly'. I pressed gently on the bush and there was a nest with a few eggs in it; I picked one up, examined it, thanked the Lord and put it back.

A presence not called God

Many people in contemporary society feel angry or disappointed with the religious institutions. When someone in this category has a numinous experience, they are not always happy to give it a conventional identification, as in the following example:

I was listening to some records, when I felt as though something had been put round me; no words can describe the feeling which filled me. I felt that some presence was with me, I had never experienced anything like it before. It was with me about thirty seconds, then it slowly withdrew, but I was never the same person again . . . if you have never experienced anything like this, you could say it was in my imagination, but if you have had such an experience, then I don't have to try and tell you what it is like, as you will know. . . . I think I should tell you that I [do not] belong to any religious body. . . . I give it no name to you, as I yet cannot give it a name myself.

The contributor of the next example is in no doubt that his experience is not of the God of conventional Western belief, yet the description is of a numinous presence:

> I . . . know that since I concluded some years ago that my mind could not accept a personal God. . . . I seem to have become more aware of this all pervading power which to me is strength, comfort, joy, goodness . . .

The dead

In many societies, religion involves a cult of the dead or of ancestors. It is tempting to speculate that, so to speak, the raw material for such a cult lies in quite commonplace human experience. Not far short of a fifth of the British population believe that they have been aware of the presence of the dead. Quite often it is a close relative, recently deceased, but the power of the Western theological tradition probably directs attention away from these experiences as a source of religious belief and, especially among the well-educated, may make them taboo. At any rate, there is research evidence from the Alister Hardy Research Centre suggesting that experiences of the dead are reported more frequently by less well-educated people. These episodes are usually given a religious interpretation (that is, it is understood that the relative returns to comfort the individual, by the grace of God). The following two examples are quite typical, though they untypically come from well-educated correspondents:

> It happened either six or seven days after the death of my mother on ——. My husband and I had that day returned home a few days after the funeral. I had just got into bed and lay waiting for my husband who was downstairs, to join me: I can't remember what I was thinking of—but I became aware that there was a warm glowing presence and I *knew* it was my mother. I heard no words spoken but I received a message from her. She told me that all was well with her and that she was very very happy. It was an almost unbelievable experience (because I don't think I really believed in life after death). I remember lying there thinking, 'I must hang on to this experience' and that I must remember it was real and actually happened and I didn't dream it or imagine it.

The next example is of a premonition of the death of a university don. The writer had been involved in nursing him while he was dying of cancer, and had gone home to bed:

> I lay on my spare room bed so as not to disturb anyone, and at 1.00 a.m. I felt his whole figure coming across the room . . . and a voice

plainly said 'He has entered heaven'. Instead of getting up and going right away I just lay there, absolutely at peace, and with a wonderful feeling of thankfulness. At 9.00 a.m. I quietly went to the house, and as the manservant met me I said 'Yes, I know . . . the Doctor has gone'. He looked bewildered, but apparently he had just passed away as I came up the drive.

A sacred presence in nature

Perhaps because of the legitimation given for such experience by the writings of the romantic poets, particularly Wordsworth, this is usually reported by well-educated people:

I had this experience in —— when I was nineteen, an undergraduate at —— University. I was reading at my desk when I looked up and out of the window at the rather dull landscape and grey luminous sky. I became aware that the sky was, I might almost say, looking at me. A mutual awareness was happening between myself and an overwhelming presence. Translated into words such as I was familiar with in the Bible this could have been stated as God calling me by name but the experience was beyond speech. After a while (I suppose again remembering the Bible) I asked, 'Is there anything you want me to do?' The answer was clear, again communicated at a deeper level than speech, 'No: only to know'. Now . . . at the age of [over 70] it remains the most memorable event in my life and I think it has provided me with a ground of confidence which so far has never failed.

Adult recollection of nature mysticism often refers back to the childhood visions studied by Edward Robinson:

As a child in the country, I wandered by myself sometimes but was rather afraid and I became conscious of solitude and silence. I became increasingly aware of a Presence which I associated with the nature around me. In my adolescence I gave It the name 'God', and aimed at being alone in communion with It.

In the same vein, sometimes reference is made to experiences that go very far back, almost to infancy. Here is another example that claims to refer to earliest memories:

I was three years old. I crouched down, as children do, very close to the ground. A black slug moved across the path, slowly, silently, leaving a shiny trail, and I sat back on my haunches to watch it. My cotton print dress circled the ground around me. Overhead the sky was blue, the sun shone . . . a tune was in my head and I hummed it. . . . There was a movement among the trees. Not the movement made by someone passing through but an overall rustle of attention as in a crowd before the arrival of royalty. Each leaf was aware, expectant. Each blade of grass alert. God was everywhere. I felt secure; held; at one with everything around me.

Evil

It is a curious fact, remarked on by the sociologist Peter Berger,[5] that at a time when religious interpretations of reality are often seen as implausible, a lot of credence is given to manifestations of evil or occult forces. Although one can hardly imagine Freud being happy with his interpretation, Berger explains this in psychoanalytic terms as evidence for the bizarre return of repressed religion. A number of the accounts have a content that is reminiscent of the staple diet of horror films, as in the following instance:

> Suddenly I became aware of a sense of the uttermost evil . . . I was enveloped by this revolting force, so vile and rotting I could almost taste the evil. I recall that I managed by a great effort to stretch out my right hand and with my index finger I traced the shape of the Cross in the air. Immediately on my doing this the evil enveloping me fell away completely . . .

The belief that supernatural evil can be combated by the use of traditional religious symbolism is also present in the next example:

> . . . I woke up one night and found myself besieged by evil, horrifying and overwhelming. I switched on the bedside lamp and looked at the clock to make sure I was awake and not dreaming. I even feel nervous about writing about it now, in bed at night. The evil was so terrifying I wondered whatever I could do to stop it and then remembered that in ancient rites one made the sign of the Cross and called on Jesus. . . . I did so more out of terror than belief but I was desperate. Gradually the evil seemed to subside.

Experiencing that all things are 'one'

As I mentioned in a previous chapter, scholars like to talk about two major categories of religious experience. The first, numinous experience, refers to those occasions when people feel that they have been in the presence of God. Mystical experience, on the other hand, refers to occasions when people feel that somehow or other they become 'one' with their surroundings. This is much more typical of people who have been through some kind of higher education than of those who have not. Maybe the former are more likely to have come across

Eastern religion, just as they are more aware of the nature mysticism of the Romantic poets. Aesthetic experience of a particularly intense kind seems to be associated with such experience, as in the following example:

> I was walking across a field turning my head to admire the Western sky and looking at a line of pine trees appearing as black velvet against a pink backdrop, turning to duck egg blue/green overhead, as the sun set.
>
> Then it happened. It was as if a switch marked 'ego' was suddenly switched off. Consciousness expanded to include, *be*, the previously observed. 'I' was the sunset and there was no 'I' experiencing 'it'. No more observer and observed. At the same time—eternity was 'born'. There was no past, no future, just an eternal now . . . then I returned completely to normal consciousness finding myself still walking across the field, in time, with a memory.

The person who gave the above account adds that, in his view, the momentary ecstasy at sunset is probably 'the most significant of human experiences between birth and death'.

Probably enough examples have been presented to give some feel for the realm of human experience that is being investigated, and the way people put it into words. The more I look at the many thousands of accounts we have in the files, the more I begin to feel that the language one uses to describe such experience is two-pronged. On the one hand, the vividness of the metaphors used by someone who has a facility with language means that the power, beauty and sometimes the terror of the experience is conveyed. On the other hand, to a degree, the metaphors are arbitrary. This comes out most strongly when one considers the classifications that have been produced. For example, in preparing examples for this chapter it has often seemed that with very little alteration the accounts could fit into many of the other categories. What I have been guided by is the language chosen by the person who sends in the account.

Three reasonably firm distinctions do seem to make themselves clear. The experience of an evil presence is quite obviously qualitatively different from all the other experiences, in that it involves a sense of horror and revulsion. There also seems to be an evident difference between the experience of a 'presence' and more mystical experiences of 'merging' with the rest of reality. But there are intermediate forms in which it is hard to be sure. Instances of nature mysticism are quite often of this type. The intensity of awareness that is so characteristic of such experience is vividly portrayed in my final example. The writer is recalling herself at the age of eight, chipping garnet crystals from a rock:

> That one day, as I was choosing which crystal to try for, the field of my vision grew brighter, a kind of dancing brightness like heat over sand, like the quite colourless light in some parts of a candle flame. All awareness of any light source vanished: there were no shadows. There was also no weight. Or mass. Each particle spread, suspended in relation to every other, first of the rock I was facing so close, which was no longer dark grey, then of this rock in relation to the other boulders behind it, then of these to the earth, of the sloping land behind it, of the globe itself. I seemed to see in and in, deeper and clearer and further. . . . I was still myself (I didn't merge) in the sense that I still saw all this from a consciousness, but it did change not only my beliefs but also my sense of bodies and material things, of independence, of holiness or value.

At least at the overt level, there is no reference here to a sense of presence, though very often descriptions of moments of intense insight such as this do become transmuted into an overwhelming awareness of a presence. But there comes a time when words are no longer adequate because the insight is blinding. The writer of the above account adds the following comment: 'Doesn't awe, inclination, or faith predetermine how much you can endure, or determine how much you have opened yourself to take in of this particular focus before it is too bright?'

Notes

1   See Tim Beardsworth, *A Sense of Presence* (Oxford: Religious Experience Research Unit, Manchester College, 1977).
2   Alister Hardy, *The Spiritual Nature of Man* (Oxford: Clarendon Press, 1979).
3   For a full account, drawn from the files of the Alister Hardy Research Centre, readers are advised to consult Meg Maxwell and Verena Tschudin, *Seeing the Invisible: Modern Religious and Other Transcendent Experiences* (Harmondsworth: Penguin Books, 1990).
4   In *Synchronicity: An A-Causal Connecting Principle* (Bollingen Series; Princeton University Press, 1973).
5   Peter Berger, *Facing Up to Modernity* (Harmondsworth: Penguin Books, 1979).

5

Widespread yet secret

A personal note

Research in the field of religion is often difficult to interpret because one is unaware of the prior personal commitments of the researcher, who may not always be prepared to be transparent on the matter. The first part of this chapter will therefore be autobiographical. It so happens that I got to know Sir Alister Hardy in the 1950s when I was an undergraduate. At the time, I was studying zoology at Aberdeen University and Hardy was my external examiner. In the summer of 1956, I managed to obtain a vacation job working on a research trawler connected with the Marine Research Laboratory in Aberdeen. Hardy was there also, collecting specimens and making watercolour sketches for a book he was writing about marine biology.

One of the routine tasks of a research trawler is to cross and recross the sea, taking sample trawls at a series of grid points every few miles. I found it very interesting to see what came up in the net, but in between times there was nothing much for me to do except sit around and wait. It was during the long lazy summer hours that I began chatting with Hardy, and in the course of our conversation discovered his lifelong interest. Nearly two decades later I found myself in Hardy's home town, Nottingham, teaching in the university, and confronted with an acute personal issue concerning religious experience.

The difficulty was that I had had some experience of this kind myself. Until the age of ten I had lived in a remote village in the north of Scotland, in what for a young child felt like a religious mono-culture. I am well aware that the decline in the religious institution was already strongly under way in Scotland during my childhood. Nevertheless, the sense of religious community in our village was still sufficiently deep-rooted for me, in early childhood, to be almost totally unaware of the existence of people who were not religiously orthodox. The one exception was my own father, whose unorthodoxy I assumed to be an acceptable eccentricity; and although he had severe criticisms of the religious institutions, I never thought of him as anything but fascinated by religion.

In such a culture one absorbs the attitudes and beliefs of the community in a very straightforward, naïve way. When I came to awareness of myself as a separate individual, among the attributes I discovered that I had already acquired was an ability to read and communicate in English and a knowledge of the Bible. As small children sometimes do, I conflated the landscape and events of the stories I read, in this case from the Bible, with the geography of the surrounding countryside. For instance, I half knew that a pool in the burn at the bottom of our road must have been where Jesus was baptized, and when reading about Moses returning down the mountain with the Tablets of the Law, I confused Mount Sinai with the hill outside our village. There is a road out of the village that, on a warm summer evening, I still think of as the road that leads to Emmaus.

Growing up in this kind of environment, it would be extraordinary if one did not have basic assumptions that are religious. I most certainly did, and continue to do so, in spite of suggestions that my faith is no more than something produced by conditioning. What is often overlooked when allegations of this sort are made is that they legitimize the counter allegation. One would also have to say that a secular culture such as many people live in today must condition them into a secular point of view. As William James said many years ago, the test of a belief is not in its origins, biological or cultural, but how it emerges from a careful examination.

In my case, the careful examination began at university when I first had to make a detailed consideration of the implications of my scientific education as a zoologist, especially in relation to Darwinian theory. It posed the classic dilemma that had faced Hardy as a student at Oxford, and which, since the middle of the nineteenth century, has faced any Westerner brought up within a religious tradition. Paradoxically, for anyone trained in the methods of empirical science, I felt that to choose the secular alternative proposed to me in my scientific education was to abandon my own direct experience, on the grounds that it clashed with somebody else's theory about the nature of reality. I was simply unwilling to ignore what my experience told me, though of course the inner controversy continued.

The private argument rumbled on until the early 1970s, by which time I was lecturing in Nottingham University. From a religious perspective, I believe that the 1970s were a pivotal time. Some of the censuring and hostility towards religion that had been a feature of my student days was beginning to seem a bit faded. The freeing up that followed released a great deal of religious energy into society, that up to that period had been suppressed or, perhaps, even repressed. It was the period when youth culture first began to include a significant, at times alarming, religious component with the rise of new cults and religious movements. As for me, in my thirties, and therefore perhaps a bit more staid, I began to have sufficient self-confidence to ask more publicly whether those scientists who dismissed religion had really looked at it with an unbiased eye.

Starting research in Nottingham

As a result, one summer term I decided to spend every spare moment between classes interviewing a random sample of students in my department. I selected 50 men and 50 women and asked them questions about direct religious experience. I am still not sure what prompted me to choose this particular course of action at this particular moment, but the findings were, at that time, quite staggering.[1]

The students I was talking with were studying for a postgraduate certificate in education; that is to say, people who had finished a university degree and intended to become schoolteachers. I started off very tentatively, inviting individuals to my office to chat. The question I used was borrowed from Hardy: 'Have you ever been aware of, or influenced by, a presence or power, whether you call it God or not, which is different from your everyday self?' I half-expected that I was about to make a fool of myself. But as the days and then weeks of interviewing passed by, I began to realize that I was on to something.

In spite of the fact that I myself had had some experience of this type, I had a lot of familiar preconceptions about people who claim they have had religious experience; it is part of the excess baggage of contemporary British culture that most of us pick up. For example, I had a stereotype of what such a person would look like. They would probably be a bit limp, a bit over-polite, somewhat old-fashioned in appearance, and probably not very bright.

I was completely wrong. Time after time, someone would come into my room and sit down; I would glance at them and inwardly say 'No, this is not the sort of person who will know what I am talking about'. It seems I had myself been taken in by the stereotypes that I so strongly dislike being applied to religion. More often than not, these unlikely people would then begin to describe vivid encounters with the sacred. As well as that, frequently the descriptions they gave were very powerful. I had not bargained with the fact that I was going to feel emotionally drained by the end of the summer.

Sixty-five out of the 100 students said that they had had some kind of religious experience, at least once or twice in their lives: 36 out of the 50 men, and 29 out of the 50 women. Only 14 out of 100 claimed to belong to a religious denomination, although a further 21 felt that in some loose sense they were 'Christian'. This seemed to mean that they were either committed religiously but disillusioned with the institutional Church, or that they had a vague residual adherence to the Christian ethic.

What did this group of young teachers-to-be talk about? Twenty-three of them felt that they were being guided or controlled by some presence or power. Twenty-two of them felt that they had had direct awareness of the presence of God. Nineteen of them had experienced an awareness of a presence in nature. Fourteen had felt a presence in answer to prayer. Ten of them had experienced a unity with nature. Another ten had had either an out-of-the-body experience or a vision, or some form of extrasensory perception. Seven of them felt that they had been aware of an evil power. However, only four felt that they had been 'converted' in the traditional Puritan or Pietist manner.

It is important to remember that when I was asking these questions, the surrounding climate, at least in popular Christian theology, was very much against either the possibility or the validity of these kinds of experiences; it was the time of the 'Death of God'. Yet I was confronted with an overwhelming majority of young graduates going into the teaching profession who knew from their own experience that there was a sacred dimension to reality. In most cases, the experience had appeared for the first time in mid-adolescence, exactly when E. D. Starbuck had found that the moment of religious conversion appeared, though some could trace back their experience much further, in the manner of Edward Robinson's informants. In most cases, they had had the experience only a few times in their lives, although a largish group of twenty claimed that they were aware of some kind of sacred presence all the time. The experience, in most cases, lasted for a minute or less; sometimes for a fraction of a second.

One of the questions I asked all of them was whether there were any particular circumstances in which the experience was most likely to occur. The commonest situation was when a person was alone or in silence, and this was closely followed by times of severe distress or decision. Universally, their experiences affected their lives in a positive manner. Immediately after their experience, the great majority said that they felt peaceful or ecstatic or joyful. Only in the case of experiences of some kind of evil presence, did people take a negative view. In the longer term, the dominant opinion was that the experience had either made the person happier or morally better, or given depth and direction to life.

Another thing I asked them was whether they themselves defined their experience religiously. About two-thirds of them said yes, and when I asked why, about half simply said it was self-evident; they *knew*. Most of the others said that it fitted with their understanding of religion, and a small number deduced that it must be religious because they could not explain it in any other way.

Of those who did not want their experience to be called religious, some said it did not fit with their understanding of religion; others said they did not believe in religion anyway; a few said it could be explained in other ways.

Working at the national level

The most significant feature for me was the unexpected richness and frequency of reportage of such experiences. The obvious thing was to write to Hardy in Oxford and tell him of my findings. The result was the setting up of the Religious Experience Research Project in Nottingham University. It was an exciting moment when the Unit in Oxford provided the money to appoint a sociologist, Ann Morisy, to work with me in developing the quantitative side of the research.

When Ann and I started to think about a national survey we began to realize how ignorant we were in this field. Friends kept asking us what we meant by 'religious experience'. Did we mean paranormal experience, that is, extrasensory perception and the like? Were we thinking of ecstatic visions, such as those described by famous saints, like St Teresa of Avila? It was one of those situations where our 'tacit' knowledge was a good deal more extensive than we were able to put into words. But the problem about tacit knowledge is that if you want to communicate with somebody about it, you eventually have to find words.

We devised all sorts of questions and spent hours freezing in the streets of Nottingham with clipboards, trying out our questions on passers-by. In the end, because it was the most successful in orienting people to the area of human experience in which we were interested, we fell back on Hardy's question: 'Have you ever been aware of or influenced by a presence or power, whether you call it God or not, which is different from your everyday self?' We then went to see National Opinion Polls Ltd and asked them to put the question to a national sample of 2,000 people in this country.

I have described the results in detail in my book *Exploring Inner Space*;[2] so I will merely summarize them here. The statistical data are presented as part of the appendix to Chapter 6 of this book. What we found was that over a third of all adults in Britain would claim to have had experience of this kind. Generally speaking, women are rather more likely to claim these experiences than men, in the ratio of four to three. As one moves up the social scale, more people will talk about religious experience; also, the more education people have, the more likely they are to talk about their experience. The happier people are, and the older they are, the more likely they are to claim experience. Most interesting of all, those who report religious experience are more likely than others to be in a good state of psychological well-being.

That survey was undertaken in 1976. The story jumps ahead now to 1986 when the Oxford Unit, now renamed the Alister Hardy Research Centre, did another survey, on this occasion using Gallup Poll. Gordon Heald (the director of Gallup Poll, London) and I asked a series of questions about the kinds of experience that I mentioned in the previous chapter. The overall total had now risen to almost half of the national population. In fact, if one includes responses claiming some sort of premonition as a religious experience, then the total rises to two-thirds of the population.

Gordon and I wrote an article about our findings which was published in *New Society* in 1987.[3] The points we were making were, first of all, that reports of experience seem to be increasing in this country and, secondly, that contrary to a lot of popular stereotypes, it is associated with a number of positive and benign factors—good mental health, good education, happiness, and social responsibility.

When the article appeared, however, we were a bit taken aback to see that whoever had decided to illustrate it had provided photographs of extreme, not to say bizarre, phenomena associated with religion. For example, there was a picture of the Austrian mystic Therese Neumann, apparently weeping tears of blood. Another picture showed St Anthony the Hermit being tempted by a voluptuous naked woman. A third showed a staring-eyed Joan of Arc hearing voices. In our article we had commented that, at least since the eighteenth century when interpretations of reality began to be dominated by rationalism, Europeans have been uncertain whether religion is the cure for a disease, or is itself the disease. We felt, rather wryly, that the contrary messages conveyed by the text and the pictures acted out this particular split in modern consciousness.

The suppression and repression of religious experience

One way the split shows itself is in what I can only call a massive taboo against speaking about personal experience of a religious nature. The shyness of people when they talk about it is very striking. In addition to the national surveys that we did, we also ran an in-depth investigation in the city of Nottingham. Using a random sample of adult citizens, we got a positive response rate which was very like that for the survey I did with postgraduate students in the university. That is to say, over 60 per cent of the sample claimed that they had had experience of this kind. This in itself suggested that some kind of self-censorship had been operating in our national surveys. People are less likely to talk about intimate personal experience during a brief interview with an opinion pollster, than they are with someone who is prepared to spend an hour or more building up a rapport, as happened in the in-depth surveys.

I became used to sitting with people in their houses, listening as they recalled the intensity and the importance of a particular experience in their lives, to the point where they could not stop crying. These very powerful experiences, I discovered, had often not been spoken about to anyone prior to the occasion on which I interviewed them. Something about the private interview situation seemed to give people permission to speak of a long-suppressed experience. In our 1986 national survey, as many as 40 per cent of people claiming experience said that they had never told anybody else about it.

Reflecting on those things that are too personal to be spoken of, we found various reasons for embarrassment. Something may be too private to be broadcast because it betrays to an outsider the tenderest secrets of an intimate relationship. In Western religion, this kind of reticence has always marked even the writings of those who, like St Teresa of Avila, have been most open and analytical about their religious experience. Another reason for embarrassment may be that something regarded as a personal weakness, probably shared with many others, but none the less a weakness, is announced to all and sundry. Or it may go further. To acknowledge certain personal experiences may involve the repudiation of a fundamental tenet of a person's central system of beliefs. Still further out on the same limb, it may amount to the exposure of secret longings or experience which may make individuals privately wonder if they are quite sane.

Following on from this, one may consider what it is that makes people consider that they will be judged by others to be stupid or mentally unbalanced. Broadly, I would guess it is the revelation of those facets of our experience which seem to be bizarrely out of tune with the everyday picture of reality presented to us by our own society.

It is the socially determined aspect of embarrassment and the fear of madness that are important here. Apart from the preservation of privacy round an intimate relationship, all the other reasons I have enumerated imply a hostile environment. In fantasy, people seem to imagine a waiting mob of sneerers, ready to ridicule them and have them certified insane if they should be unwise enough to reveal their secret.

The most obvious defensive measure is simply to keep quiet about it. But at times I think people go further. It is as if they suppress the possibility of religious experience by an act of will. My favourite example of this comes from a young member of a revolutionary political group who had an almost Lenin-like violence in his antipathy to religion: it disgusted him. Yet at times he confessed, as we all must, to moments of weakness. It was then that he sometimes found himself on the edge of prayer, only to draw back with stern admonitions to himself about the meaninglessness of such an act. Perhaps the mere intellectual acknowledgement that religious experience is an impossibility can be enough to suppress its appearance.

Then there is the question whether people might push the religious dimension of their experience right out of consciousness, as suggested by Peter Berger. And in fact, there is a whole complex of imagery at the heart of popular culture that implies a repression of religion among ordinary people. For several years now the supernatural, officially a realm of fantasy, has often been presented as being dominated by the absolutely evil. Some of the classics of the horror movie genre, films like *The Exorcist* and *Omen* or *The Amityville Horror*, portray the supernatural as flesh-creepingly loathsome. A few years back, a number of pop groups specialized in names implying that they were religious outcasts, like Judas Priest, Black Sabbath and The Damned. If this kind of displacement were to take place in the realm of sexuality, Freudians would be quick to interpret it as the bizarre and distorted return of something real, something that at the conscious level has been denied.

Why the avoidance?

But why should people go to the length of denying their religious experience? After all, there does not, at least in the West, seem to be any kind of attempt formally to censor the expression of religious *belief*, and even in the Soviet Union the attack on religion has been in decline of late. Public figures even make obeisance to it from time to time, averring to their constituency that it is a 'good thing'. Births, marriages and deaths continue to be celebrated or mourned over in churches and Christian prelates are given a public hearing.

The answer lies in a much more profound influence on the way we conduct our lives, hiding beneath the surface layer of cosy religious chit-chat. It is so pervasive that it hardly enters the reflective consciousness of most people. I mean, of course, the heritage of nineteenth-century positive science. Everyday science, even in the late twentieth century, is still not the tentative and sophisticated stuff of modern philosophers of science; a bread-and-butter version informs the basic assumptions, not only of people in the street, but of the average worker in a research laboratory—as I know personally, having worked in one for some years.

This latter brand of science has developed protective mechanisms that enable it to explain anything and everything in its own terms —and of course this amounts to unwarranted superstition. Just as followers of the occult believe that everything—literally every-thing—that goes on in the world can be explained by it, so hardboiled positivists re-explain all supposed experiences of the transcendent in terms of the immanent. And the basic assumption most of us live with permanently, if not *de jure* then *de facto*, is that all real events are explained exhaustively in terms of immanent causes.

Often the brilliance of the material achievements that have flowed from an apparent application of this philosophy is contrasted in people's minds with the supposed ineptness and corruption of the religious institution, and regular announcements regarding the implausibility of its documentary sources and doctrines. This, combined with a physical decline of the Church in Europe, seculariza-tion, gives the claims of transcendence a fragility and insubstantiality which, especially to the uncommitted observer of religion, make it seem totally vulnerable to the cold winds of reality.

It is within this context that modern industrial men and women meet with, and have to interpret, those experiences that I have been calling religious. They carry within a part of them the knowledge that such experience simply isn't on; in fact, they are in the position of someone backing their experience against the whole weight of the culture in which they were nurtured.

Back in 1963, an American psychologist, Stanley Milgram, published a research article[4] showing that ordinary people will obediently perform what appear to be horrifying experiments on their fellow human beings, simply because a 'scientist' in a white lab coat requests it. They feel unable to refuse such an authority figure. It must be obvious that the much larger step of refusing to accept the interpretations of reality held by a dominant scientific culture requires either remarkable self-confidence or the presence of a protective ghetto.

We therefore seem to have the necessary conditions for the creation of a taboo. First, it is clear from our research that religious experi-ences are nearly always highly valued. Not uncommonly, they are seen as a source of meaning and the basis of moral behaviour; in fact, as the pivotal events of life. Along with the very high evaluation of these experiences is the powerful social prohibition we have just been discussing. They are therefore both desired and forbidden, sacred yet illusory, the source of both meaning and madness. In this way, rather oddly transmuted, the industrial West has recovered the great original taboo, which early anthropologists used to define as 'The Sacred, perceived ambivalently as both holy and dangerous, pure and impure'.

The attitude of the churches

Those people brought up within the mainline Christian churches are used to hearing stern warnings against paying too much attention to the experiential aspect of religion. Among Protestants this is often associated with the influence of Karl Barth. Within Catholicism, similar warnings are given against taking too much interest in the phenomena of mysticism. That is not what true religion is about, we are told.

No doubt there are commendable reasons for this, connected with the necessity for care in discriminating between reality and illusion. It also derives from the writings of classical mystics who were concerned that religious aspirants should not be diverted from their path by becoming obsessed with the phenomena they encountered. But the context out of which these people wrote was very different from our own. They lived in the midst of societies which, by and large, had few doubts about the religious interpretation of life. Among their pupils there must have been many who were curious about the phenomena of mysticism in an empty way, not concerned to relate them to a coherent pattern of religious development. No doubt, moderns have an equal penchant for empty curiosity, but popular versions of reality fail so miserably to take account of the whole range of human experience that the first step must surely be to create a space in which fleeting, puzzling, but deeply moving personal experience is taken seriously.

If Alister Hardy is right—that these experiences are part of being human, have always been there, and indeed are a major root, or *the* major root, of religion—then their widespread survival is no surprise. When institutional religion is going through a phase of decline, as is currently the case in Britain, what one would expect is that while other aspects are in retreat, the central and most powerful root is the one that lingers on most strongly. In other words, the postulated experiential beginning is the irreducible basis on which religious interpretation is built.

As a result of historical circumstances, interpretations come and go; at one moment in history they seem highly plausible and gain massive assent from large numbers of people. But times change. New moods and new information bring a feeling of declining plausibility to old ways of understanding, and consequently they suffer a partial or complete eclipse. However, while the eclipse is going on, the root does not wither. It remains widespread, though largely invisible.

It may be that if you, the reader, are from a relatively orthodox Christian background and have persisted with my argument thus far, it is with a growing sense of irritation at my failure to take theology, and in particular the doctrine of Grace, seriously. I believe that, on the contrary, I am defending it. For reasons that historians of culture must disentangle, people outside the religious institutions live in a society that makes them schizoid about what they themselves half accept are the promptings of Grace. They know about their experience, yet they dare not admit it or give it the value they would wish. This hiddenness and secretiveness is due to a latter-day scholasticism of science (often colluded with by religious people who seem to lack confidence in the value of their deepest heritage), which asks people to forget and deny their own depths. These are often the most powerful memories in a person's life, the moments when meaninglessness and alienation from the rest of the world were removed, or hope appeared in a desperate situation. In such circumstances of intellectual and cultural isolation, it is not surprising if people construct a private theology, remote from and eccentric in relation to orthodox religion.

It is not without significance in conjunction with this to note the occasions on which religious experience commonly manifests itself. It is almost never in a church or with other people. Rather, it tends to be when a person is deeply distressed or, alternatively, quite alone. These are moments when cultural censorship loses its power and immediate experience comes home to the individual. Out of this comes the need to interpret one's experience in a way that does justice to it, and it is here that the subtlety and interpretative strength of religious symbols begin once more to reveal themselves. For some people, these symbols have never lost their plausibility. For others, it is as if their experiences *in extremis* or in solitude give them the strength to break an interdiction.

Those who bemoan the decay of religious organizations are often extraordinarily opaque to the strength of experiential sources of religious motivation. I say this in full awareness of the success of the charismatic movement, because I have in mind those who are not temperamentally in tune with it, or who are well outside the bounds of it. Perhaps this blindness is the result of a concern to begin with the specific, historical kerygma. But the discursive expression of religion in sacred books and doctrinal statements has been the subject of the fiercest large-scale criticism for over 200 years in the Western world. The alienation of ordinary people from the institutions is the fruit of that critique; as Cardinal Newman might put it, it has 'poisoned the wells'[5] from which we draw our genuine and deepest inspiration. However, if, lying within many of these alienated people, there is already an empirical starting point, perhaps that is where the proclamation also begins.

The common experience

Religious experience has always been pivotal in what might be called the Pietist traditions of Protestantism, which have their critics among fellow Christians as well as from those of a secular persuasion. I myself am unhappy at what I perceive as a temptation to social passivity and political conservatism in contemporary Pietism. But it need not necessarily be so, nor was it so in the past, as a study of the role of Methodism in the labour movement quickly demonstrates. In their anxiety to play down experience, critics often forget its ubiquity, not only in Christianity, but in many, if not all, religious cultures. Descriptions of religious experience, or mystical experience, form the centrepiece of a vast corpus of literature, East and West.

To illustrate how widespread such experience is in all branches of Western religion, it is only necessary to refer to the contents of a popular work such as F.C. Happold's *Mysticism*.[6] His examples of people who know religion in its experiential dimension include some of the very greatest heroes of religion:

> Plato, St John, St Paul, Plotinus, Dionysius the Areopagite, St Augustine, St Bernard of Clairvaux, Richard of St Victor, Dante, Meister Eckhart, Blessed John Ruysbroeck, the author of the *Theologia Germanica*, Thomas a Kempis, the author of *The Cloud of Unknowing*, Walter Hilton, Julian of Norwich, Nicholas of Cusa, St Teresa of Avila, St John of the Cross, Thomas Traherne, William Law, Richard Jefferies and Pierre Teilhard de Chardin.

Adolphe Tanquerey's *The Spiritual Life*,[7] until recent years a standard text in Roman Catholic seminaries, directs the religious novice to over 300 writers, adding that only the most important authors are mentioned. The enthusiast is referred to Pourrat's three-volume *Christian Spirituality*[8] for more detail.

Within Catholicism, the term 'religious experience' is rarely used in theological works, for the simple reason that it originated in Protestantism. Something like the same area of experience is covered by the term 'mysticism', which again has a different meaning within Catholic theology from its use by students of comparative religion. There is in fact a chaos of overlapping terminology as one moves through different religious and scholarly traditions. Nevertheless, it is at least arguable that a common universe of discourse is being hinted at, not merely in the classics of Christian spirituality, whether Protestant, Catholic or Orthodox, but also in the realms of Jewish, Islamic, Sikh, Hindu and Buddhist 'mystical' writing, as well as what we can glean from so-called 'primal religions'. This 'common core' view is not very popular with professional students of religion at present. They say that when one examines religions closely, it becomes clear that the detailed statements made in classical texts differ so much from each other at the logical level that they couldn't possibly be talking about the same thing.

The problem about classical texts, from whatever tradition, is that they have the function of sustaining an orthodoxy, and they explain what the religious novice must expect as his or her experience develops. Structuring of interpretation will be particularly strong in the case of someone who follows a clearly predetermined tradition, say as a Christian or Buddhist monk. But powerful structuring of the interpretation of experience doesn't lead us to deny the reality of a common ground for it, any more than differences in language between people from different countries lead us to say that, in more than a metaphorical sense, they don't inhabit the same world as us.

If religious awareness is something natural to us, as I believe it is, interpretation will vary in exactly the same way as interpretation of any other human experience. What we find in the great religious cultures is that such awareness is taken account of and built into the fabric of life in a way that is constructive for both the individual and the community, providing society with its meanings, its coherence and its values.

What has happened in modern industrial cultures such as our own is the loss of a coherent interpretation for this realm of experience, so that it is very poorly integrated into everyday life, with a resulting loss of meaning and value. Nevertheless, as the research work of the Centre has repeatedly shown, the experience is still there, extraordinarily widespread, and, so to speak, in search of understanding. It would seem to me that much of the craziness or extremism associated with modern religious cults is a reaction to the denial of our religiousness. Once our currently tabooed experience of the sacredness of reality is accepted as normal, there is some chance that it can be integrated into, and integrate, our fractured sense of community.

Notes

1   David Hay, 'Religious experience amongst a group of post-graduate students: a qualitative study', *Journal for the Scientific Study of Religion*, vol. 18(2) (1979), p. 164.

2   (2nd edn; Oxford: Mowbray, 1987).

3   'Religion is good for you', *New Society* (17 April 1987).

4   Expanded into a book entitled *Obedience and Authority* (London: Tavistock Press, 1974).

5   This phrase was Newman's rejoinder when Charles Kingsley accused him of dishonesty, thus paradoxically denying Newman the possibility of defending himself honestly. See John Henry Newman, *Apologia pro Vita Sua* (first published 1864; republished London: Fontana, 1959).

6   *Mysticism: A Study and an Anthology* (Harmondsworth: Penguin Books, 1970).

7   *The Spiritual Life* (New York: Desclee & Co., 1930).

8   P. Pourrat, *Christian Spirituality* (3 vols; trans. S. P. Jaques; London: Burns Oates & Washbourne, 1930).

6

An American parallel

The United States: Greeley and McCready

When the Alister Hardy Research Centre first began its research, the staff were unaware of anybody else doing similar investigations. We rather imagined that the last people to do significant work in the field were William James and his pupil E.D. Starbuck, at the turn of the century. We then discovered that almost in parallel with ourselves, two Americans, Professors Andrew M. Greeley and William C. McCready, were already doing similar work at the University of Chicago. Greeley, now professor of sociology at the University of Tucson in Arizona, is somewhat unusual in that he is a Catholic priest who is also an eminent sociologist. In his very readable monograph *The Sociology of the Paranormal*,[1] he talks of how his interest in the field of mysticism developed.

Most certainly it was not when he was a young seminarian. As he says, little was heard in those days about mysticism, save for an occasional warning from a zealous spiritual director to be wary of the self-deceptions involved in religious experience. At the time, the warning seemed pretty pointless to Greeley, because, whatever else could be said about it, the atmosphere of the seminary was not particularly conducive to religious experience. Nor when he was working as a parish priest in Chicago did he expect to find much in the way of mysticism.

Again, the place where one might expect to come across religious experience was not Greeley's starting point. It was during a piece of sociological research in the 1960s that he more or less stumbled across the fact that a number of the people he had interviewed spoke about such experiences. One of his colleagues had suggested inserting a question about it into a survey; when the results came in, the proportion of respondents reporting the experience was quite high. As he and Bill McCready were both working at the National Opinion Research Center (NORC) at that time, they had the opportunity to investigate this further. They had to contend with the same kind of split view of the world that exists on this side of the Atlantic. Greeley quotes the following from the psychiatrist Mortimer Ostow as characteristic of a certain kind of scientific view:

> Confronted with an inacceptable reality, intra-psychic, personal or social, the individual turns his back on that reality, excluding it from his consciousness and psychically destroying it. He replaces it with a new inner reality which he has so designed that it gratifies rather than frustrates him. This process represents a rebirth, a return to a state of mind characteristic of his infancy, when he was able to deal with frustration and disappointment by retreating to a world of fantasy, and when he was blessed with a firm and intimate union with his parents.

That Ostow's view is not out of character for the psychiatric profession becomes clear when one examines the latest edition of the *Diagnostic and Statistical Manual of Mental Disorders (DSM-3-R)*[2] published by the American Psychiatric Association in 1987. This is the standard handbook for psychiatric diagnosis in the United States. Among the eight criteria, any two of which suffice to identify either the prodromal or the residual phase of a schizophrenic disorder, are: 'Odd or bizarre ideation, or magical thinking, e.g. superstitiousness, clairvoyance, telepathy, "sixth sense", "others can feel my feelings", over-valued ideas, ideas of reference. Unusual perceptual experiences, e.g. recurrent illusions, sensing the presence of a force or person not actually present.' In the diagnosis of what is called schizotypal personality disorder, the same criteria are used, with the addition of an example of what is meant by sensing the presence of a person not actually present—'I felt as if my dead mother were in the room with me'. Another criterion of schizophrenic disorder is the manifestation of 'extreme perplexity about one's own identity and the meaning of existence'. In another type of mental illness, manic disorder, 'God's voice may be heard explaining that the individual has a special mission'.

Neither Greeley and McCready, nor I, would dispute the fact that the phenomena described may be useful in diagnosing mental illness. Nevertheless, there is a severe problem of discrimination, since *DSM-3-R* notes: 'Beliefs or experiences of members of religious or other sub-cultural groups may be difficult to distinguish from delusions or hallucinations. When such experiences are shared and accepted by a sub-cultural group, they should not be considered evidence of psychosis.' That is to say, phenomena that are acceptable when they occur in a cultural context that gives permission for them, become criteria for the diagnosis of insanity when they are manifested outside such a group.

Sometimes the unsupported presupposition of pathology becomes quite bizarrely overt in supposedly objective scientific papers. Thus, for example, in a 1983 paper on religious and mystical experiences as 'artefacts of temporal lobe function', M.A. Persinger explains the importance of his work on transient electrical micro-seizures (TLTs) in the temporal lobe of the brain as follows:

> First, these portions of the brain are also correlated with bursts of aggression . . .; since the sense of personal meaningfulness is an intricate [sic] component of religious experiences, is there a genetic propensity to kill with the conviction of cosmic consent following specific types of TLTs? Second, many acute religious behaviours are correlated with opiate-like complacency, helplessness, and the expectation of divine deliverance; how would the decision-making patterns of people who occupy powerful political positions be influenced by TLTs during the threat of self-annihilation?[3]

Perhaps the nervousness that Greeley detected in his seminary days arises from the kind of intemperate language that a very long line of scientific commentators on religion choose to use. If, as he says, the Roman Church presides absent-mindedly over the oldest mystical tradition in Western history, perhaps the absent-mindedness is because its caretakers want to forget it, in the face of such an onslaught.

Fortunately, Andy Greeley is one of the most determined figures in the world of American sociology, so he is inclined to take this sort of thing as a challenge. The assumptions that he and Bill McCready made were:

1 That they should take ecstatics at their own word that their experience is cognitive; that is, that through the experience they gain knowledge. If they say that they see, then it is up to psychologists of perception to find out just what perceptual phenomena are involved. Philosophers and theologians can give a commentary on whether what ecstatics think they see is really the way things are. Greeley and McCready chose to examine the phenomenon itself, and whether the mystical experiences are breaking through to ultimate reality, or merely a psychotic episode, is not their affair.

2 They wish to define ecstatic experience as 'religious'. They do not intend it in the formal ecclesiastical sense, but with the signification given to it by a number of social scientists: that religion is a set of symbols that purport to provide a unique interpretative scheme to explain the nature of ultimate reality. Mystics don't have to go to church to be religious, or to profess a doctrine. It is their cognitive experience that is religious.

3 Ecstatic experiences are going to be like all other experiences in that they have their antecedents in the person's past. That is to say, they will be affected, like every other experience, by the person's upbringing and, particularly in the case of these experiences, by the quantity and quality of the religious life of the parents.

4 That experiences of this kind will powerfully affect attitudes and behaviour. In other words, people who have had an experience of this kind will behave differently and have different values from people who have not.

5 They assumed that ecstatic experience was not particularly infrequent in American society. Just because social scientists have not got around to examining a phenomenon, this does not compel us to conclude that the phenomenon does not exist.

The final point that Greeley and McCready made was that it depends on what one's original explanation of religious experience is, how one will predict the sort of person who reports experience of this kind. One could in imagination portray ecstatics as oppressed, unhappy, rigid people looking for reassurance and release, which their interlude of self-induced withdrawal (*qua* Ostow) provides. Alternatively, one could see the ecstatic as someone who has had a peak experience that releases, perhaps temporarily, the most creative and generous of human resources.

Greeley and McCready's findings

The NORC survey was carried out in 1973 and Greeley and McCready found that 35 per cent of American adults claimed to have had a religious experience. The question they used, 'Have you ever felt as though you were very close to a powerful spiritual force that seemed to lift you out of yourself?', was very different from Hardy's. Yet we know (because Ann Morisy and I used Greeley and McCready's question in the same 1976 British survey as the one in which we used that of Hardy) that people who say 'yes' to the former question will almost certainly say 'yes' to Hardy's. The impression one gains is that there is a common area of human experience that people know perfectly well, but they use a wide array of culturally determined verbal expression to refer to it.

When one thinks of the sheer numbers implied by the results of the American survey, the proportions are impressive. According to the results, in the early 1970s something like 70 million Americans would have been willing to admit that they had experienced this kind of interlude and ten million of them would claim to have had such

experiences frequently. Proportionately, that is much the same fraction of the population as would have made a similar claim in Britain at
that time, though the distribution is not quite parallel. (Over the past
twenty years there has been at least a dozen large-scale surveys of
reports of religious experience in Britain, the United States and
Australia. In a brief book it is not possible to enter into a detailed
examination of the figures, but the more important statistics are
summarized in a set of tables forming the Appendix to this chapter.)

In the United States, unlike Britain, reports of experience are
approximately as common among the young as among the old.
Another striking finding for Greeley, in his role as a Catholic priest,
was that Protestants are much more likely to report such experiences
than Catholics. My own view is that the form of the question asked
has a very powerful effect on the way that the person will respond.
Greeley and McCready's question, although posed by sociologists
who happen to be Catholics, is actually rather Protestant in style,
inquiring as it does about personal experience not necessarily
mediated by ritual.

Let me illustrate this a little further. If one chooses to ask a random
sample of the population the question 'Are you saved?', as street
evangelists are fond of doing, it is much more likely that somebody
with a Protestant Evangelical background will respond positively than
will a Roman Catholic. The medium through which religious
experience most prominently manifests itself among Evangelical
Christians is conversion, being 'born again', or being 'saved'. This is
the rhetoric of Protestantism, but it does not imply that members of
other groups, religious or non-religious, do not have any religious
experience. It may simply be that their experience is mediated
another way, most obviously in Catholicism through ritual and
sacrament; or in the case of other religious groups through the
language and customs of their own culture; in non-religious groups
perhaps it spills over through delight or ecstasy in such things as
music, poetry, sexual intercourse, or natural beauty.

One of the most interesting questions that Greeley and McCready
asked people about was 'triggers' of mystical experience. In an earlier
chapter I expressed my misgivings about references to triggers as if
they were the cause, rather than the occasion, of religious experience.
Nevertheless, with that proviso in mind, I would like to quote from
Greeley and McCready's list of triggers, and provide illustrative
examples drawn from the files of the Alister Hardy Research Centre.

The most frequent category mentioned in the NORC survey was
listening to music. Forty-nine per cent of those who had had an experience mentioned this as a trigger. Here is an example from a young
man in his teens, where the doctrinal content is minimal, yet the
mood is without doubt religious:

One warm summer afternoon I was lying on my bed, face down, listening to a recording of Sibelius' Violin Concerto. My eyes were closed and the only thing that was entering my consciousness was the tremendous music. When the Concerto came to an end, I got up from the bed and looked out of the window to see the whole world transformed. Everything was bright, vivid, trembling with life. It seemed that I was being given a vision of the beauty of creation.

Another example drawn from the files describes a response to the music of Bach, which has a much greater overt theological content:

A friend persuaded me to go to Ely Cathedral to hear a performance of Bach's B Minor Mass. I had heard the work, indeed I knew Bach's choral works pretty well. I was sitting towards the back of the nave. The Cathedral seemed to be very cold. The music thrilled me . . . until we got to the great *Sanctus*. I find this experience difficult to define. It was primarily a warning. I was frightened. I was trembling from head to foot, and wanted to cry. Actually I think I did. I heard no 'voice' except the music; I saw nothing; but the warning was very definite. I was not able to interpret this experience satisfactorily until I read—some months later—Rudolph Otto's *Das Heilige*. Here I found it: the 'numinous'. I was before the Judgement Seat. I was being 'weighed in the balance and found wanting'. This is an experience I have never forgotten.

Greeley and McCready's second category of trigger is *prayer*. Unlike most other categories which, so to speak, are involuntary, in this one there is obviously a positive attempt to lay oneself open to experience:

I came to the end of my tether one day and realized that only God could help me. I prayed and as I could not feel any contact made myself persevere. I realized my prayers all my life had only been lip service. I spent more and more time each day in prayer, and one day I suddenly felt the breakthrough. I knew I was in touch with a spiritual being. My prayer for help really came from my heart, mind and soul, for the very first time. After some time, I felt a warm glow on my head. Very slowly it spread until my whole being was suffused with it. I kept my eyes closed so don't know if there was any visual accompaniment. Gradually, the glow subsided and I rose to my feet. Then the strangest thing happened. On both my shoulders, was firm pressure as of unseen hands. I was guided to a bookcase and my right hand involuntarily reached out and I selected a book. I opened it and from the pages fell a text cut from a newspaper . . . 'All things whatsoever ye shall ask in prayer, believing, ye shall receive.'

The next commonest trigger was *the beauties of nature*, perhaps associated with a particular spot; what is notable again is the earliness of this memory:

One such place has a significance for me beyond all others. A mile or so from —––, the heath fell away to the estuary of the [river] —––, a few sparsely clothed Scotch firs along its banks. To the left, —–– Church crouched austerely above the few cottages that are the remnant of the flourishing medieval port. And in the far distance, beyond the firs, gleaming against the dark sky, the white fleck of —–– Lighthouse. This scene, lovely enough, but not uniquely so, became at some point a window through which my childish sensibilities—I must have been about four at the time—glimpsed a still beauty that I have since come to recognize as the most powerful and awesome experience of my life, different not just in intensity, but in kind, from any other . . .

The next category is *moments of quiet reflection*. Once again, the example comes from early childhood:

My father used to take all the family for a walk on Sunday evenings. On one such walk, we wandered across a narrow path through a field of high, ripe corn. I lagged behind, and found myself alone. Suddenly, heaven blazed on me. I was enveloped in golden light, I was conscious of a presence, so kind, so loving, so bright, so consoling, so commanding, existing apart from me but so close. I heard no sound. But words fell into my mind quite clearly—'Everything is all right. Everybody will be all right.'

The writer of the above, now in the latter part of her life, connects her comment with the famous quotation from Mother Julian of Norwich, 'All shall be well, and all shall be well, and all manner of thing shall be well'.

The next commonest category is *attending a church service*. The following example probably typifies the commonest of all religious experiences in relation to church going:

Over the years the Mass, and particularly the Holy Communion, has provided the kind of religious experience for me which I think you are seeking. That is a depth of reality, an understanding of life and of people, a heightened awareness of good and bad, of beauty, of suffering. Words are very inadequate to express this kind of experience, particularly if it covers a period of time. The only analogy I can suggest is to consider one's eyes previously to have been covered with an opaque substance and gradually layer by layer having this removed. [One discovers] the value of life, of love, of God.

Next is *listening to a sermon*. Some of the most vivid examples of this relate to response to the preaching of an evangelist, as in the following instance:

I listened to the sermon and it was if some power beyond myself took hold of me and spoke to me. The words spoken seemed for me alone and when we were asked to go forward to dedicate our lives to Christ *nothing* and I mean *nothing* could have held me back. I wish to impress very strongly to you that it was not emotional feeling alone or mass hysteria as some say. I was just drawn by a power beyond myself and I felt my great need. Afterwards I felt a great peace and joy that I can't put into words. It was, and still is, a miracle to me.

The next category is *watching little children*. The example I choose comes from someone who was affected by more than simply the youthfulness of the person she was with:

About this time I began working part-time among mentally and physically badly handicapped children. There was a particular child who was totally helpless in mind and body, and in constant pain. One morning I saw him and felt more than usually distressed and disturbed by him. On my way home, I was thinking about him in relation to the Creator of things (God?)—and I suddenly saw everything in its true proportion—the smallness of man's life and lifespan and the immense otherness of the force outside us. I can still recapture the extraordinary impact of this idea as it came to me then (by great concentration) but I can never adequately express it.

Next is *reading the Bible*. Sometimes, at the moment of reading, the power of the words seems to spring from the page. On other occasions, as in this example, the effect of the words comes later:

Once, when I had been reading John 12, verse 24 and 25, 'I tell you, most solemnly, unless a wheat grain falls on the ground and dies, it remains only a single grain; but if it dies, it yields a rich harvest. Anyone who loves his life loses it; anyone who hates his life in this world will keep it for the eternal life.' And I went for a walk in some pine woods alone. It was a glorious spring day and I stopped for a bit under a pine tree and looked at things. Quite suddenly those verses became full of a new depth of meaning and everything I saw in nature around me glowed with this meaning and truth for the whole of life, mine included.

The final category I will illustrate is *being alone in church*:

For me there is something extraordinary about the stillness of ancient churches, especially those in remote places. They seem to symbolize the most profound part of us that is waiting to be rediscovered. Once, sitting in the northernmost of our great churches, surrounded by the red glow of the ancient stone, I found myself opening a Bible at the place where God asks Job 'Where were you when I laid the foundations of the earth?' The total context engendered such a sense of religious awe, that the only adequate release was tears.

Opening up to the sacred

There are other sub-categories in Greeley and McCready's list that I have not given examples for, including reading a poem or a novel, childbirth, making love, creative work, looking at a painting, and physical exercise. All of them seem plausible occasions for the transcendent moment—even the last category, physical exercise, which is reported by only 1 per cent of Greeley and McCready's sample. One only has to remember the experience of Eric Liddell to understand that it can indeed occasion a sense of the transcendent.

But primarily, what I think we are looking at is not exactly 'triggering', but the moments when someone's consciousness becomes more deeply aware of reality. If we look at the culture we belong to, it is clear that there are particular occasions when such experience is, so to speak, 'supposed to happen'. When we listen to marvellous music, or still ourselves in prayer, or are entranced by the beauty of nature, or are passionately in love with someone, our awareness is raised, both by the situation itself and by the expectation that our culture engenders in us concerning such moments. Nevertheless, religious experience has occurred in every conceivable human context, including the grimness of a slum, in a concentration camp, on a rubbish dump, on a battlefield, in the midst of torture, during the conduct of a scientific experiment, in a business office, during radiation treatment for cancer; in fact, it is impossible to find any human situation whatsoever where such experience could not occur—indeed, has not occurred.

On examination of the secular culture in which we live, what one encounters is a narrowing of vision caused by social taboo. Much more interesting than triggering, is to remind oneself again of the occasions when this taboo is broken. One of the points that turned up very early in the examination of the accounts of experience that were sent in to the Alister Hardy Research Centre is the number of them that seem to be associated with times of great personal distress. This was so striking that in our in-depth survey in the city of Nottingham, we took care to monitor this particular point. It became clear that around 50 per cent of all the accounts we received were associated with a time of disturbance, such as the loss of a loved one, the loss of a job, the fear of death, or severe bodily injury. If religion is something deeper than an intellectual matter, if in fact it is something extremely primitive and profound in us, there may be an explanation for this.

Most of the time we are pressured by the society to which we belong into certain ways of understanding the world. Partly this is learned in school, partly it is learned from our parents and teachers, but mainly we learn it from the attitudes that we pick up from the media and what is happening in society in general. For a very large number of people, most of the time, life is lived at second hand, very remote from an appreciation of direct, here-and-now experience. It is characteristic of all the major religions that they try to point this out to people and suggest that it is important to become more aware of reality.

It is when people are up against it, when things seem very bad, that they are, so to speak, forced to take reality seriously at last. The vividness and pain of their experience brings it strongly into focus. By definition, religions concern themselves with the whole of reality. What is being avoided when the intense reality of direct experience is side stepped is perhaps the religious depth of human experience. Hence, in a secularized world, the unavoidable intensity of personal suffering may be the occasion for such reality to burst upon the individual.

The other very striking discovery at the Alister Hardy Research Centre is how very frequently these experiences occur when one is alone. Perhaps it is the case that exactly the same forces operate here. Once I am away from my fellow human beings it is true that my mind can meander endlessly into the past or the future. Nevertheless, there is not the pressure to conform to a given picture of reality. Could it be that on such occasions, our normally suppressed awareness becomes heightened?

Values

Probably the most important piece of information uncovered by Greeley and McCready is an association between religious experience, well-being, and concern for the well-being of other people. American mystics are more likely to be happy, well balanced, less likely to be racially prejudiced than other people. This is backed up by another piece of research done by Professor Robert Wuthnow,[4] now in the sociology department at the University of Princeton. He found in a study of a large group of people in the San Francisco Bay area of California, that people who claimed 'peak experience', which includes religious experience, were also more likely than others to be concerned about the welfare of other people, less likely to be concerned with the accumulation of material wealth.

These research findings are potentially of great importance because they suggest that there may be, so to speak, an empirical link between morality and religion. But the link is not directly with the religious institutions as such; it is more to do with a personal discovery of what might be called a religious perspective on life. How this works out in practice can be illustrated by an account sent in to the Alister Hardy Research Centre by someone recollecting the day her life changed. At the time she was a young secretary in the entertainment industry, fed up with the tawdriness she saw around her. One evening she decided to take a break:

> It was a glorious sunny evening and I walked through the park and sat down by the water intending to read. I never opened my book. It was very beautiful with the sun glinting through the trees and the ducks swimming on the water, and quite suddenly I felt lifted beyond all the turmoil and the conflict. There was no visual image and I knew I was sitting on a seat in the park but I felt as if I was lifted above the world and looking down on it. The disillusion and cynicism were gone and I felt compassion suffusing my whole being, compassion for all the people of earth. I was possessed by a peace that I have never felt before or since, and—what is to me most interesting and curious of all—this whole state was not emotional; it was as if I was not without emotion but beyond it . . . The experience passed off gradually, and I suppose it lasted about 20 to 30 minutes. At the time I felt it was an experience of God, because I interpreted it according to my own religious framework.

Following this incident, she left her job and took up a career as a social worker dealing with delinquents.

Having read many accounts with this kind of outcome, I still find it difficult to make a generalization about how this ethical follow-on is generated; there are very many variations on the pattern. In the above case, which probably could serve as an approximate model, it seems to relate to a loss of the 'psychological distance' between the individual and the rest of reality. Even if only for a moment, people feel they have discovered the true state of affairs—we are part of everything and everything is part of us. This is possibly easiest to see in mystical experiences or numinous experiences that have a mystical element, of which I give another example. It occurred when a young man, on holiday in Scotland, was climbing near Ben Nevis:

> I was climbing first and was ahead of my companions. The roar of a waterfall nearby was deafening, until I climbed over the rim of the rock face. In absolute quiet, within a beautiful scenic panorama, I found God. The description of Samadhi fits my experience perfectly. I was no longer aware of 'myself'; and yet I retained my personality. This was however merged into an infinite corporate personality of all life. Peace, love and understanding became real and tangible.

Nevertheless, a parallel realization emerges from purely 'numinous' experience. This is sometimes expressed as the direct discovery that we and our environment are all the creation of God, thus engendering a sense of responsibility or stewardship for the whole of the given reality.

The most salient feature of this is what I have called the empiricism of the discovery. To the person who has had the experience it seems a self-evident physical fact that to do damage to any element of the delicate fabric of reality, whether it be other people, other living creatures, or the inanimate world, is in some deeply intimate way to damage ourselves. Of course these intuitions often pass in a short time, sometimes a fraction of a second, and they are forgotten or ignored; nevertheless, the recollection of them stirs the conscience. What *is* the case is that the experience leads us to know that we *ought* to behave morally in relation to the rest of reality. The motivation of members of groups concerned with the defence of the poor, with justice for political prisoners, or racial and social minorities, or the environment, or attacking the madness of the arms race, or opposing sexual discrimination, may very often be traced back to experiences of this sort.

The repeated finding that religious experience has an empirical link with ethical behaviour suggests that it is not wild speculation, but down-to-earth common sense, to give freedom for it at the centre of modern culture. Critics of the very real cruelties and injustices perpetrated by religious institutions, now and in the past, often fail to recognize that the departure of the churches from justice and mercy is a departure from their wellsprings in religious experience. This is not a reason to outlaw religion, but to cleanse it.

The disintegration of a sense of value, of self-worth, of meaning —which is at the root of many of our ills—for large sections of the population, particularly young people, has certainly got economic and political causes which must be tackled at the political level. But I do not believe the crisis will be solved by political change alone. It also requires the releasing of inner resources which ultimately are ethical and, from a traditional perspective, religious. This is the single biggest challenge facing the churches and the educational system today.

Notes

1 Andrew M. Greeley, *The Sociology of the Paranormal: A Reconnaissance* (Sage Research Papers in the Social Sciences, Studies in Religion and Ethnicity Series no. 90–023; Beverly Hills and London: Sage Publications, 1975).

2 *Diagnostic and Statistical Manual of Mental Disorders (DSM-3-R)* (3rd edn—revised; Washington: American Psychiatric Association, 1987).

3 M. A. Persinger, 'Religious and mystical experiences as artefacts of temporal lobe function: a general hypothesis', *Perceptual and Motor Skills*, vol. 57 (1983), p. 1255.

4 Robert Wuthnow, *Peak Experiences: Some Empirical Tests* (Berkeley: University of California, Survey Research Center, 1976).

Appendix   International statistics

The statistical tables presented below have been compiled from national poll data collected in Britain, the United States and Australia during the past two decades, on the frequency of report of religious experience and associated demographic and social data. On the whole, the tables are self-explanatory. For detailed analysis, readers are referred to the original publications which are given in the list of sources at the end of the Appendix.

Table 1   Positive responses to questions about 'religious experience' in eleven national surveys

Survey	Publication date	Nationality	Sample size	Proportion claiming experience
Back and Bourque (Gallup)	1970[a] (1962) (1966) (1967)	USA	3,232 3,518 3,168	20.5% 32% 41%
Greeley (NORC)	1975	USA	1,467	35%(G)[b]
Hay and Morisy (NOP)	1978	Britain	1,865	36%(H)[b] 31%(G)[b]
Gallup	1978	USA	3,000	31%
PRRC[c]	1978	USA	3,062	35%
Morgan Research[d]	1983	Australia	1,228	44%(H)[b]
AHRC/Gallup	1985a	Britain	1,030	33%(H)[b]
AHRC/Gallup	1985b	USA	1,525	43%(H)[b]
Hay and Heald/Gallup	1987	Britain	985	48%

Notes:
a The 1970 publication refers to Gallup surveys conducted in 1962, 1966 and 1967.
b H = response to Hardy question; G = response to Greeley question.
c Princeton Religion Research Center.
d Morgan Research is the Australian associate of Gallup International.

Table 2 Frequency of positive response compared with age for six national surveys

USA	Teens	Twenties	Thirties	Forties	Fifties	Sixties	Seventies
Greeley (1975)	32%	33%	33%	38%	43%	36%	35%

USA	Under 30		18–24	25–29	30–49	50+	
Gallup (1978)	31%		27%	39%	32%	29%	

BRITAIN	16–24	25–34	35–44	45–54	55–64	65+	
Hay and Morisy (1978)	29%	35%	33%	36%	43%	47% (Hardy question)	
	25%	28%	26%	31%	33%	42% (Greeley question)	

AUSTRALIA

	16–24	25–34	35–44	45–54	55–64	65 +
Morgan Research (1983)	42%	41%	44%	50%	45%	44%

BRITAIN

	16–24	25–34	35–44	45–64	65 +
AHRC/ Gallup (1985b)	25%	31%	35%	36%	34%

USA

	18–29	30–49	50 +
AHRC/ Gallup (1985b)	36%	47%	42%

Table 3 Report of experience compared with education for seven national surveys

USA		*Amount of education*			
		1–8 years	*9–12 years*	*Technical*	*College*
Back and Bourque (1970)	1962	21.7%	19.6%	20.0%	20.4%
	1966	34.0%	29.3%	30.8%	33%
	1967	48.5%	37.5%	34.3%	38.3%

BRITAIN		*Education to:*				
		13–14	*15*	*16*	*17–19*	*20 +*
Hay and Morisy (1978)	(Hardy question)	37%	29%	37%	44%	56%
	(Greeley question)	31%	24%	30%	35%	50%

USA	*Grade school*	*High school*	*College*
Gallup (1978)	30%	31%	29%

AUSTRALIA	*Education to:*				
	13–14	*15*	*16*	*17–19*	*20 +*
Morgan Research (1983)	37%	47%	40%	48%	45%

USA	*No high school grades*	*High school grades*	*College incomplete*	*College graduates*
AHRC/Gallup (1985b)	37%	39%	47%	50%

Table 4 Report of experience compared with social class for four national surveys

	Hay and Morisy (1978)	Gallup (1978)	Morgan Research (1983)	Gallup (1985)
Upper middle class	47%	—	—	—
Professional/middle	49%	39%	50%	44%
Lower middle class/ white collar	41%	33%	42%	35%
Skilled working class	31%	31%	31%	29%
Unskilled/subsistence	32%	29%	49%	28%

Table 5 Report of religious experience in Britain, according to claimed religious adherence (Hay and Morisy (1978))

Anglicans	33%
Non-conformists	44%
Roman Catholics	41%
Other Christians	68%
Jewish	39%
Other non-Christians	60%
Agnostics	23%
Atheists	24%
Don't know	23%

Table 6 National frequency of report of different types of experience (Hay and Heald (1987))

Total positive response:
48%

Types:

Patterning of events	29%
Awareness of the presence of God	27%
Awareness of receiving help in answer to prayer	25%
Awareness of a guiding presence not called God	22%
Awareness of the presence of the dead	18%
Awareness of a sacred presence in nature	16%
Awareness of an evil presence	12%
Experiencing that all things are 'one'	5%

Table 7 Percentage saying 'No' in answer to the question 'Have you told anyone else about your experience?' (Hay and Heald (1987))

Awareness of a sacred presence in nature	44%
Awareness of receiving help in answer to prayer	42%
Experiencing that all things are 'one'	40%
Awareness of kindly presence looking after/guiding	39%
Awareness of the presence of God	38%
Patterning of events	33%
Awareness of the presence of someone who has died	28%
Awareness of an evil presence	28%

Table 8 Percentages of people interpreting their experiences religiously (Hay and Heald (1987))

Awareness of the presence of God	80%
Awareness of receiving help in answer to prayer	79%
Awareness of a sacred presence in nature	61%
Awareness of kindly presence looking after/guiding	58%
Experiencing that all things are 'one'	55%
Awareness of an evil presence	38%
Awareness of the presence of someone who has died	35%
Patterning of events	32%

Table 9 Percentage of people reporting the experience taking place when they were alone (Hay and Heald (1987))

Awareness of receiving help in answer to prayer	76%
Awareness of the presence of someone who has died	75%
Experiencing that all things are 'one'	69%
Awareness of kindly presence looking after/guiding	68%
Patterning of events	66%
Awareness of the presence of God	64%
Awareness of a sacred presence in nature	64%
Awareness of an evil presence	61%

Sources

Back, K. and Bourque, L. B.	(1970) 'Can feelings be enumerated?', *Behavioral Science*, vol. 15, p. 487
Gallup Poll	(1978) *Religion in America: The Gallup Opinion Index 1977–8* (Princeton: AIPO)
Gallup Poll	(1985a) '4 in 10 Americans have had unusual spiritual experiences' (Princeton: AIPO press release)
Gallup Poll (with AHRC)	(1985b) Unpublished national poll of reports of religious experience in Britain
Greeley, A. M.	(1975) *The Sociology of the Paranormal: A Reconnaissance* (Sage Research Papers in the Social Sciences, Studies in Religion and Ethnicity Series no. 90–023; Beverly Hills and London: Sage Publications)
Hay, D. and Heald, G.	(1987) 'Religion is good for you' (report on a Gallup National Survey of religious experience), *New Society* (17 April)
Hay, D. and Morisy, A.	(1978) 'Reports of ecstatic, paranormal or religious experience in Britain and the United States: A comparison of trends', *Journal for the Scientific Study of Religion*, vol. 17(3), p. 255
Hay, D. and Morisy, A.	(1985) 'Secular society/religious meanings: a contemporary paradox', *Review of Religious Research*, vol. 26(3), p. 213
Morgan Research	(1983) Unpublished national poll of reports of religious experience in Australia
PRRC (Princeton Religion Research Center)	(1978) *The Unchurched American* (PRRC/AIPO)

7

The need to break a taboo

The social reality of religious experience

I have noted the suspicion that religious ways of experiencing reality have their roots in social or individual illness. The practical effect of this critique has been to create a taboo that alienates people from their spiritual experience and their awareness of their unity with the rest of creation. In my estimation, the unhappiness this has created in terms of personal emptiness and a damaged social fabric is very great.

For many people, the criticism of religion has been expressed most clearly and convincingly by two figures who have influenced this century with great power, Karl Marx and Sigmund Freud. I, in turn, wish to criticize their views on religion, but I will be seriously misunderstood if I am seen to be making a general attack on their opinions. However much their stances have since been adapted, argued over or contradicted, the very force with which they entered into European history implies that, even if only obliquely, they have struck a chord of vivid recognition in matters of religion.

In the 'Contribution to the Critique of Hegel's Philosophy of Right', Marx stated his axiom, 'The basis of irreligious criticism is *Man makes religion*, religion does not make man'. Later, he uttered his most famous and moving corollary, '*Religious* distress is at the same time the *expression* of real distress and the *protest* against real distress. Religion is the sigh of the oppressed creature, the heart of a heartless world, just as it is the spirit of a spiritless situation. It is the *opium* of the people.'[1]

If 'religion' refers to the social, doctrinal, ritual and ethical dimensions of human beings' response to their experience of the sacred, then I cannot see how one can deny that there is a broad strand of truth in Marx's assertion. Since these dimensions of religion are humanly propagated, they can be humanly corrupted. Marx's righteous anger at the widespread use of religion during the nineteenth century as a means of oppressing people or controlling them is akin to the anger of the Old Testament prophets.

Yet Marx never addresses the dimension of religious experience out of which the prophets claimed to speak and which, from the biological perspective argued in this book, is the most crucial issue. Marx's silence, one presumes, is because he felt he had already dealt with the substantive issue. If so, one can make the plausible assumption that he would have conjectured that such experience is no more than an extreme example of false consciousness; in this case, the fantastic imaginings brought on by the sufferings of members of the most oppressed sectors of class-society. This is a conjecture that is scientifically testable.

Freud paid direct and serious attention to religious experience, which he believed to be symptomatic of neurosis; some of his less inhibited followers would go further and claim it as at least temporarily psychotic in nature. The plain fact is that among people claiming to have had religious experiences, there are indeed some who are distinctly odd, apparently caught in a private world of experience which, to an outsider, is very remote from reality. The validity of Freud's insight has been used creatively by today's students of religious experience as a guide to discriminating between what they would see as genuine experience, leading to maturity, and fantasy generated by an infantile return to what Freud called the 'pleasure principle'.[2]

But Freud seems to have extrapolated further from his encounters with the fantasy, to make an inductive generalization which has much to do with his theoretical and philosophical position on the nature of religion. His well-known conclusion is that religion is the 'universal neurosis'. Again, in so far as it refers to religious experience, this conjecture is scientifically testable.

My contention is that the functional critiques of religion may have some validity in relation to institutional religion to the extent that it has become corrupt, and in relation to religious experience in as much as some who claim it are manifestly insane. In relation to the experiential roots of religion in the general population, though, these critiques are seriously mistaken. Furthermore, I assert that this can be demonstrated in an orthodox manner, using arguments proposed by the philosopher of science Karl Popper.[3] My claim is based not only on data presented in earlier chapters, but on a wider range of evidence than can comfortably be presented in a short book. For those who are interested in more detailed statistical data, reference can be made to the Appendix on pp. 79–85, which summarizes the important research findings of the past twenty years.

Most people, even those who have had a scientific education, tend to think that the task of the scientist is to explain, very directly, how the world works. Scientists, it is said, solve puzzles by examining a phenomenon closely, suggesting an explanation, then trying to prove that the explanation is correct by doing a repeated series of experiments to demonstrate it. This sounds like common sense and, having myself worked in a research laboratory, I know that many scientists persist in thinking that is what they are doing, in spite of Popper. But, says Popper, they are mistaken. One can never prove the truth of a scientific explanation by using the so-called 'inductive method', because the facts we observe could fit any number of hypotheses.

Some of the most massively obvious inductions in human history have been proved incorrect. Thus, I can propose the hypothesis that the sun goes round the earth and I can suggest an infallible way of testing it. I and my fellow observers get up early every morning and watch the sun rising over the eastern horizon, note it crossing the sky, and carefully observe it going down in the west. It would seem that my hypothesis has been overwhelmingly proved by the fact that this has happened every day of my life. Nevertheless, for other reasons, primarily the addition of new information, for several hundred years we have ceased to accept this hypothesis as the simplest way to interpret the data.

What we *can* do, says Popper, is suggest daring hypotheses to explain what we perceive and test them in an attempt to *dis*prove them, because one contradictory result is all that is needed for disproof. A famous logical parallel to this process is the discussion of the induction that 'all swans are white'. We may notice that all the swans we have ever seen are white and therefore make the induction that if a bird is identified as a swan, it will always be white. However, it takes only one instance of the discovery of a black swan (such as the species to be found in Australia) to prove that the induction is wrong.

Popper's views have been the subject of vigorous debate, and I do not myself want to restrict rational scientific studies to those instances of research that follow the strict canons he lays down. Nevertheless, the investigations I have been describing abide by the demarcation criterion on which he vigorously insists, in that they test the conjecture or hypothesis that religious experience is pathological. At least in relation to religion that is rooted in the kinds of experience I have been discussing, the data contradict that hypothesis in the following ways:

1 Taken at face value, the Marxist thesis that religion (and therefore religious experience) is symptomatic of social pathology predicts its predominance among the poorest and most oppressed sectors of society; at least in Britain, the reverse holds true for religious experience. Only by manufacturing amendments that reverse the force of the original hypothesis (for example, by claiming religion as the mode in which alienation manifests in the dominant classes in society) can the thesis be maintained.

2 The data that have been assembled on the psychological well-being of populations reporting religious experience contradict the view that religious experience is associated with poor mental health. The statistical significances are in the opposite direction. People reporting such experience are *more* likely than other people to be in a good state of psychological well-being. Curiously, Freud was already aware of this in his own psychiatric practice. His response to the fact that religious people do not exhibit individual neurotic symptoms as frequently as other people was to class religion as a 'crooked cure'. But once the origins of his argument are seen to lie in a philosophical assertion about the nature of reality, its circularity as a scientific thesis becomes obvious. In Popper's terms it does not pass his demarcation criterion because it is impossible to refute it.

3 In an earlier chapter I commented on the ambivalence of the sociologist Emile Durkheim over the 'reality' of religious experience. Alister Hardy was convinced that he was not trying to explain it away, but to put it in terms that did not do violence to his scientific convictions. Others have thought Durkheim's explanation of religious experience as the 'effervescence' generated in large religious gatherings was a dismissal. There is no need to come to a decision on one side or the other of this debate, because research at the Centre indicates that in any case the hypothesis is not sustainable. The great majority of religious experiences that have been studied in random sample surveys by the Centre took place when the individuals reporting them were completely alone.

Even claiming the authority of the Popperian method for the assertion, and supporting the findings of the Alister Hardy Research Centre with available data from numerous other research organizations and universities in the United States and Australia, it would still be arrogant in the extreme to claim that this by itself refutes the broad intellectual stance of an intellectual establishment that is dominant and has widespread credibility. Nor would I claim that such investigations could or should, in themselves, support in a positive sense the credibility of religion. Research of this type can make no statement about ultimate reality. What it *does* do is to alter quite radically the informational base out of which our understanding of the contemporary religious phenomenon is constructed.

It poses questions to the secular establishment, whose views have played a major part in precipitating the continuing crisis of plausibility in which religion finds itself. This crisis is commonly said to be the result of a growing rationality in the way we conduct our affairs. But there is now sufficient historical distance from the initial impact of secular ideas to exercise some discrimination in the matter. Great as were the insights of such figures as Marx and Freud into certain forms of religion, their views also depended on an ignorance of, or perhaps avoidance of, straightforward empirical evidence such as I have referred to. Intense commitment to a scientific or political belief can (like intense religious belief) generate an insensitivity to the total human condition that contradicts the avowed intention of the scientific method.

Taking religious experience seriously

One can make a guess that social phenomena that are more or less universal must have some functional importance in maintaining the fabric of society. This is frequently asserted of religion, though secular beliefs such as humanism, Marxism, or a trust in psychoanalysis or the scientific method are said to do the same job. The latter differ, of course, in that they have on the whole ignored or attacked religion's concern with the sacred, and in this respect I claim that they fail to do justice to the reality of the human condition, as revealed by modern empirical research. Should that be so, they cannot in the long run succeed in their integrative role, unless they adapt—as I think began to happen to some degree during the 1960s in, for example, certain reformulations of 'Eurocommunism'. The prominence of religious motifs in the disturbances now occurring throughout Eastern Europe perhaps indicates that even those were insufficient.

It is highly unlikely that the vast array of religious expression spread across the world and throughout history is purely and simply pathological fantasy, or a device for the maintenance of a *status quo*. Nor is it plausible to explain religion as a purely theoretical exercise in meaning construction. On the contrary, in most places for most of history, religion is taken to be the most direct and practical of human activities, dealing as it does with the fundamental questions of human experience and existence. Accordingly, those who specialize in transactions with the sacred—priests, monks, nuns, hermits, shamans and the like—are usually accorded high status in their communities.

The interesting thing about these findings, as far as my argument is concerned, is the link there appears to be between report of religious experience and personal wholeness. Sensitivity in this dimension seems to parallel sensitivity in other dimensions of human experience. In other spheres of life, phenomena that are widely reported and are associated with human well-being are usually thought to be 'natural', 'part of being human', and steps are taken, at least in just societies, to see that their benefits are spread to as wide a range of people as possible. Not only is this not the case with regard to religious awareness, but most people are excessively shy about confessing that they have even had such experiences. They wonder if they have deluded themselves, and they usually fear that if other people find out about it, they will be ridiculed or thought insane. While it is true that there are religious forms of insanity, the data to which I have been referring in this book make it clear that, on the contrary, religious experience is associated with sanity and wholeness.

Rationalism and the numinous

I am not competent to make an informed judgement on how the long-standing and increasingly powerful rejection of the religious dimension of life came about. It would involve explaining the rise of modern European culture and that is a task for the encyclopaedic skills of a cultural historian. Perhaps, at some future date, a coherent body of scholarship will develop out of the many attempts, sociological and historical, to interpret the process of secularization, which I interpret as a wedge driven into the manifold of human experience so that it is artificially split into sacred and secular parts. Meanwhile, the basis for my stance is a stubborn determination to trust the validity of my own and other people's direct experience. Until the arrival of the requisite act of scholarly dedication, I mention tentatively some straws in the wind, illustrative of the ideas that I find explanatory.

It has become a cliché to talk of a movement in European history called the Enlightenment, which it is claimed began some time in the seventeenth century, conveniently labelled by the publication of Francis Bacon's scientific work *Novum Organum* in 1620. As I understand my historian colleagues, a more accurate interpretation of the matter would suggest that between the beginning of the seventeenth and the end of the eighteenth century there appeared, untidily in the midst of many other ideas, a series of insights that most of us now believe were indeed 'enlightening' for Europeans.

At one level it is possible, by judicious selection, to illustrate the progress of the Enlightenment as a steady and coherent increase in the dominance of a secular, rational and empirical model of reality. This sort of description identifies the impetus for the movement in the scientific revolution, with Copernicus, Galileo and Newton as its heroes. Some of the key notions as they have come to affect our understanding of religion are as follows.

First, human reason is supreme. We discern the truth of any situation by directly consulting our reason. The most famous English philosophical representative of the Enlightenment, John Locke, proposes that the lover of truth does not hold to any proposition with greater assurance than the proofs it depends upon will warrant.

'Whoever goes beyond this measure of assent, it is plain . . . loves not truth for truth's sake but for some other end.' One of the apparent implications of this for traditional Christianity is that reason must have priority over what the Bible says, or the authority of the Church.

It would be an error to suggest that the use of reason was not important before the arrival of Enlightenment ideas, but it altered in its functions. Instead of being used to construct a body of religious and philosophical truths on the basis of logical argument, its operation was turned more and more to the interpretation of the results of scientific investigation. People were becoming much more interested in nature as something to be investigated by scientists. The idea that nature is uniform and arranged in an orderly manner made people expect that whatever they found out would apply universally. Where a particular religious system claimed to be true, but was thought to be so by only one section of humanity, reflective people began to doubt whether the truths that it claimed could be considered fundamental. Following the model of science in which 'truth' is gradually discovered and ever changing, no truth could ever be so absolute as to justify the suppression of contrary views by force. For example, it would not be right to enforce one kind of religious uniformity in one place (London, Geneva, Rome) while denying it in others.

The immediate result of these developments was not, on the face of it, to damage religion, but to cause it to be seen in a much more rational light. One of the acknowledged founding fathers of Enlightenment thinking was Lord Herbert of Cherbury, who flourished mainly in the early seventeenth century and has been called the father of Deism. He argued in his book *De Veritate*, published in 1624, for a natural religion which could be agreed upon by everyone, regardless of historical differences between faiths. Everybody, thought Lord Herbert, had certain innate ideas imprinted in their minds by God. These included a knowledge that God exists, has a right to be worshipped, that virtue is the chief part of the worship of God, that crime is evil and we should repent our sins, and that there will be rewards and punishments after death.

Although Lord Herbert claimed that his religion was based on reason, he certainly did not wish to deny the possibility of some form of religious experience. In fact, he attests in his autobiography to the validity of publishing *De Veritate* on the basis of a religious experience. He tells of making the decision via the following prayer:

Oh thou Eternal God, author of that light which now shines upon me, and giver of all inward illuminations, I do beseech thee of thine infinite goodness to pardon a greater request than a sinner ought to make; I am not satisfied enough whether I shall publish this book,

De Veritate, if it be for thy glory I beseech thee give me some sign from heaven, if not, I shall suppress it.

Lord Herbert continues:

> I had no sooner spoken these words but a loud though yet gentle noise came from the heavens (for it was like nothing on earth) which did so comfort and cheer me, that I took my petition as granted, and that I had the sign I demanded, whereupon also I resolved to print my book: this (strange so ever it may seem) I protest before the Eternal God is true, neither am I in any way superstitiously deceived herein, since I did not only clearly hear the noise, but in the serenest sky that ever I saw, being without all cloud, did to my thinking see the place from whence it came.

In the 'rational supernaturalism' of John Tillotson (1630–94) it is possible to see a second, political motivation for religious rationalism. Tillotson became Archbishop of Canterbury at a time when the establishment felt threatened by Puritanism. He was keenly and anxiously aware of the explosive potential of the religious 'enthusiasm' of the Puritans, as well as more radical dissenting sects. They claimed to have come upon politically revolutionary ideas on the basis of religious experience. Their extravagances often sounded like madmen's talk of a particularly dangerous kind to the rational and reasonable Anglicans then in the seat of power.

Like most other Anglicans, Tillotson did not deny the reality of revelation, and he might have felt some sympathy with the mysticism of the Cambridge Platonists of his time. Unfortunately, the political situation was sufficiently unstable to disincline establishment figures from having any truck with mysticism, which they wrongly tended to equate with the 'enthusiasm' of the Puritans.

Towards the end of the seventeenth century John Locke published his *Essay Concerning Human Understanding*. As a practising member of the Church of England, Locke had little time for what he saw as the wild excesses of religious 'enthusiasm'. The explosiveness of this movement at that time was perhaps not too remote from the intensity of some of the large-scale religious movements that we see influencing world politics around us today.

For Locke, enthusiasm was a fallacious ground for assent to a proposition, because it 'takes away both reason and revelation and substitutes . . . the ungrounded fancies of a man's own brain . . .'. 'Enthusiasts are those who cannot be mistaken in what they feel . . . they are sure because they are sure, and their persuasions are right, only because they are strong in them.' But, adds Locke, 'to examine a little soberly this internal light and this feeling on which they build so much: the question here is, how do I know that God is the revealer of this to me; that this impression is made on my mind by His Holy Spirit and that therefore I ought to obey it?'

Locke's writings were commonly interpreted in Europe as an attack on religion and were later to inspire some of its great secular critics, such as the Scottish rationalist David Hume. Locke had quite clearly in view the behaviour of members of the dissenting sects, and it is sometimes forgotten that he had a religious purpose in criticizing the enthusiasts. Reason is useful, he says, to criticize those who claim a Divine origin for any mad fancies they have, but it can also be used to test more serious claims to revelation since 'revelation can never be contrary to reason'.

At one point in his essay, Locke says that God only occasionally reveals a truth to man; nevertheless, 'by the voice of His Spirit' he does so from time to time. On occasion he goes to what his rationalist supporters must have considered injudicious lengths to protect this possibility. In his *Second Vindication of the Reasonableness of Christianity* he even claims to know something of the guidance of the Spirit in his personal efforts to discover the true meaning of Scripture. These experiences, he claimed, had made it indubitable to him that God does speak to human beings and that the knowledge given is more certain than any other kind.

Changing metaphors

Nevertheless, it is generally conceded that Locke was a central figure in the age of reason and a forerunner of modern secular ideas. Along with it there arose a fundamental change in the form of language used, especially in its metaphors.

The radical transcendence of God was a major theme of the Reformation, particularly in its Calvinist form, although it has also been traced back by some writers to biblical Judaism. The argument runs somewhat as follows: in an age that came to insist strongly on reason as the only source of truth, God became so remote from the daily concerns of this world that, for all practical purposes, human beings were on their own. Eventually, in a secular version of this stance, individual human beings discovered themselves to be radically alone in a world from which God had entirely departed. In that moment their language finally began to take a secular turn because their primary preoccupations were, by force of circumstance, also secular.

Religious metaphor has not by any means disappeared, even from modern everyday language, but for most people, including quite a number of theologians or otherwise formally religious people, its referent has become steadily thinner. The Victorian poet Swinburne's lines in his *Hymn to Proserpine*, 'Thou hast conquered, O pale Galilean; the world has grown grey from thy breath', could successfully ignore the incredible richness of historical Christian culture only because secularism had advanced so deeply and destructively into the religion of his time. Religion had lost its vividness and taken on much of the wilted effeteness and deadening orthodoxy that Swinburne rightly detected.

Gradually, a new set of images for reality became more dominant, though the faded metaphors remain, even today. Thus people will often speak nowadays about 'this world' as opposed to the 'other world', which is where everything spiritual resides. But they have great difficulty hanging on to the spiritual side, because—as all of us have been taught in school—'really' the world is made up of particles and space. Then, because matter is so basic, we are inclined to see our conscious awareness 'as if' it were 'superstructure', built on, as a rather fragile extra, to the more fundamental material reality. The universe is easily thought of 'as' a machine, and by analogy we can think of our brains 'as' machines—or more correctly, nowadays, 'as' computers. God, if he still exists, is 'outside' the system. However, since we 'know' that consciousness is superstructure, maybe we should search 'below', in the material world, rather than 'above', for an explanation of its contents, including religious beliefs.

The most basic, naïvely primitive religious stance is to perceive the world as pervaded through and through by a sacred presence. Such an attitude is most vividly presented to us within Christianity in someone like Francis of Assisi. With the development of the rationalism I have described and its metaphors which, at a minimum, force a chasm between God and creation, there must have arisen a suspicion of this way of experiencing reality, expressed as a fear of pantheism or fetishism. Eventually it would generate the idea that to perceive the sacred in all things is something superstitious or childish.

Another influence must have been the philosophy of Descartes with its insistence on the primacy of clear and distinct phenomena as the proper data for scientific investigation. All-embracing encounters with sacred reality, which fail to yield to objective measurement or discursive account, would thus tend to be abandoned as outside the bounds of a competent empiricism.

Once these mechanical models of the universe were conceived of, and religious ways of experiencing reality were seen in this light, they removed themselves from being the most *directly practical* of all human experiences, to being the most *remotely theoretical* of our mental constructions. Religion's importance would then become functional rather than profoundly explanatory, and it could be maintained only on the grounds of expediency, that is, as a comfort, as the ethical cement of society, etc. In this kind of intellectual climate, the weakness of the rationalism of critics like Marx and Freud, in that they are prevented by their philosophical presuppositions from making an adequate investigation of religious experience, becomes veiled from us. All they had to do was to demonstrate a dysfunctional role for religion as alienation or neurosis; an easy enough task, since the objective was to explain what was already interpreted as a mistake.

The steady loss of plausibility of religion would naturally be accompanied by increasing corruption of the Church, because officials of the institution, not being in any way immune from the processes occurring in society, would behave in a more and more cynical way. They would thus give a further twist to the spiral of implausibility. This mood in society would have the following consequence. For those whose attitude to religion is isolated from, and therefore has no basis in direct experience, critiques of the type I have been describing (along with the great historical conundrums of religion such as the problem of evil, and the modern criticism of the literary and traditional sources) would have great power. Since to them religion is merely a manifestation of superstructure, there is no reason for doing what one would naturally do in science; that is, to attempt a reformulation of the interpretative framework that continues to respect the basic human experience. To the extent that such experience continues to be allowed a certain reality, it is explained in terms that reduce it to 'nothing but' illusion, false consciousness, psychosis, etc.

The need to recover inner space

The crudity and abbreviation of the personal reflection I have presented should not be allowed to put off those who are much better informed than I in the fields adverted to. In a way, I am setting an agenda, and the essence of my case is that, somehow or other, the culture we belong to has come to act as a powerful censor of our religious awareness. Once people are convinced there are sound theoretical reasons to dismiss it as illusory, religion tends to be pushed out of consciousness or, if it does manifest itself, it has to be interpreted away as an aberration.

Thus a majority of children, when they arrive in school for the first time, will already have assimilated many of the concepts that underpin this dismissal. They will have some feeling that the sacred books of the religions are really fairy stories, that religious people are out of date and a bit silly, that clergy are figures of fun. All of this will have been picked up from a multitude of cues within the family—coyness in speaking about religion, sentimental talk at

Christmas time that equates religion with belief in Santa Claus, contempt for the hypocrisy (real or imagined) of religious officials, and the equation of religion with fanaticism and political reaction. Where children do not carry these assumptions inside them, it is because they have been brought up in an enclave that is struggling against the weight of secular pressure.

In 1977 two sociologists, Bernice Martin and Ronald Pluck, published a report of a study they had done on the religious dimension of belief among teenagers.[4] One of their most striking findings was the virtual absence of a coherent religious perspective among those they interviewed. Only 2 out of a sample of 100 were attached to any kind of religious movement, and they belonged to what sounds like a fundamentalist Christian sect. The comments from the teenagers suggested a view of religion as part of the mythology of childhood: 'It's just part of growing up. You get beyond that stage. At about 12 or 14 years old religion just wore off.' Martin and Pluck added:

> . . . childhood belief is breached with incredible ease on the basis of a simplistic scientism. . . . What takes over is a vocabulary and ambience of empirical science . . . the scientific vocabulary asks for 'facts' and 'proof', and seeks to reduce all the stories of conventional religion to scientific formulae. But it can encompass without so much as a blink of the eye ghosts and poltergeists . . . exorcism, superstition, belief in luck and fate, the use of horoscopes, the reading of tea-leaves, the efficacy of crosses and Bibles against hauntings. And time and time again it is 'open-minded' to the point of credulity about Martian spaceships as the 'true' 'scientific' source of early religious beliefs. In short, any sort of idea, however fantastic, will be given house-room if it can be dressed up in a scientific or, more accurately perhaps, a 'science fiction' garb.

The authors' explanation for this apparent chaos lies in the loss of plausibility of the traditional 'meaning-giving' institutions in the midst of the complexity of modern society. In the end, they say, individuals are left to their own devices, culling scraps and oddments of meaning here and there from the complex and contradictory world around them.

Martin and Pluck's research was undertaken at approximately the same time as the national surveys by the Alister Hardy Research Centre were beginning to reveal that religious experience is reported very widely in Britain, even among young people. Since then, a survey of over 6,500 teenagers in Britain and Ireland, reported by Edward Robinson and Michael Jackson in 1987,[5] revealed that nearly 80 per cent felt they recognized in themselves something of mystical experience. Robinson and Jackson's study was not conducted with a rigorously selected random sample of teenagers, so too much must not be made of their findings. Nevertheless, taken with the national survey data, there is a puzzling discrepancy with Martin and Pluck's results that needs to be explained.

First, the methodology of Martin and Pluck's research was to interview a group of young people, brought together for the purposes of the research, and ask them to talk about their beliefs and attitudes, particularly those to do with religion. In view of the taboo against speaking about religious experience that has been repeatedly demonstrated, I interpret the findings as at least in part being due to the use of an inappropriate style of investigation. Group discussion, especially with the sorts of peer pressure typically felt by teenagers, is almost certainly not the best way to scrutinize the private world of religious belief and experience.

Secondly, the thesis of teenage incoherence is not necessarily correct. What I discern in the descriptions offered is the clear voice of European positivism. Here is Auguste Comte,[6] positivist, and one of the founding fathers of modern sociology, writing in the early nineteenth century: 'each one of us . . . does he not remember that he has been successively, with regard to his most important ideas, *theologian* in his infancy, *metaphysician* in his youth, and *natural philosopher* (scientist) in his manhood?'

The teenager quoted earlier could easily have been the young Comte; his statement is almost identical. Similarly, in the quotation from Martin and Pluck, it is true that the religious institution is nowhere to be seen. But an orthodoxy that *does* provide plausibility, though wildly and naïvely expressed by the young people interviewed, is very much present; it is there in the guise of 'science', which is mentioned seven times by the authors in a brief paragraph.

Thirdly, in the same paragraph, one can perhaps see suppressed or repressed religion forcing its way out in the form of superstition and a curiosity about the occult. One may ask whether religious understanding for a large proportion of the population is somewhat in the position of a primitive and superstitious form of science, with much credulity in evidence and very little in the way of a coherent background of theory. The research I have discussed makes it likely that, at some level, most people, even the most ill-educated, are privately convinced that they have a religious dimension to their experience. The problem is that they have neither social permission nor the necessary language to articulate it so that it sounds coherent or acceptable to religiously orthodox ears.

It is here that I believe we can see the influence of 'folk theology', as the sociologist of religion Robert Towler describes it.[7] Folk theology does not appear in textbooks; it is passed on informally within particular groups in society. In my view it is an error to chart the decline of the Western religious institution as the one true indicator of secularization. An alternative account, supported by the findings I have discussed in this book, is to say that religious interpretations of human experience are by no means disappearing. The fact that these 'theologies' are unsophisticated, naïve and superstitious means that they tend to be ignored by investigators. But they are there, mostly kept secret, in what is perceived to be a hostile environment.

The task of the churches, if they wish to minister to the spiritual needs of the majority of the British people, must be to become more sensitively aware of this hidden religion.

Notes

1 See Marx and Engels, *On Religion* (Moscow: Progress Publishers, 1972). A very readable overview on this subject is David McLellan, *Marxism and Religion* (London: Macmillan, 1987).

2 See André Godin, *Psychological Dynamics of Religious Experience* (Birmingham, Alabama: Religious Education Press, 1985). Also W. W. Meissner, SJ, MD, *Psychoanalysis and Religious Experience* (Yale University Press, 1984).

3 Karl Popper, *The Logic of Scientific Discovery* (London: Hutchinson, 1959).

4 Bernice Martin and Ronald Pluck, *Young People's Beliefs* (Church of England Board of Education, 1977).

5 Edward Robinson and Michael Jackson, *Religion and Values at 16 +* (Alister Hardy Research Centre and the Christian Education Movement, 1987).

6 Auguste Comte, *Cours de Philosophie Positive*, quoted by E. E. Evans-Pritchard in *Theories of Primitive Religion* (Oxford: Clarendon Press, 1965).

7 Robert Towler, *Homo Religiosus* (London: Constable, 1974).

8
The way ahead

We live today in an agnostic age. Its nearest parallel perhaps is the situation in the first two or three centuries of the Roman empire, when the Graeco-Roman polytheism had lost its hold and then, as now, many people were looking to the East to find a more satisfying world outlook. Nevertheless, even today, firsthand religious experience continues to occur, not only in the traditional religious denominations, but outside as well.

Professor H. H. Price

Science as the intention to understand

In 1985, shortly before he died, Sir Alister Hardy was named before a group of eminent scientists and churchmen at the Church Centre of the United Nations in New York, as the winner of the Templeton Prize for progress in religion. The award was made to Sir Alister in recognition of the pioneering work of the Unit that he had set up, and which was renamed in the same year the Alister Hardy Research Centre. Its purpose is to make a disciplined study of the nature, function and frequency of report of first-hand religious or transcendent experience in people today.

The decision to work at the boundary of science and religion, just as William James, E. D. Starbuck and Estlin Carpenter had chosen to do at the beginning of the century, was a risky one. The research at the Centre tends to be seen as too scientific for religious people and too religious for scientists. This raises the important and fundamental question as to whether it is possible to make a valid scientific study in this field.

One thing a scientist, *qua* scientist, can never do is to enter the realm of transcendent experience itself. That is why science cannot possibly be used to disprove the truth of religion, and why claims that 'science has disproved religion' are misplaced. Attacks made on the validity of religious belief in the name of science are not scientific at all, but implicitly philosophical. What scientifically minded critics of religion often do is to try to back up their philosophical presuppositions by claiming to demonstrate that the effects of religion in the 'real' world can be seen to be bad—that is, result in social injustice, personal unhappiness, the obscuring of truth, and the like.

The attack on religion in the name of science turns out to be unscientific and usually based on a prior personal conviction that religious belief is a pernicious error. To enter into scientific research with prior beliefs of all sorts is inevitable, and not a particular problem if one is aware of them and makes them public. Difficulties arise in the study of religion when someone mistakes a personal prejudice for a hard fact, and, for example, sets out to provide a 'reductionist' explanation of another person's religious experience; in other words, by 'reducing' it to some phenomenon that *is* acceptable to them, such as a neurotic upwelling of the contents of the 'unconscious'.

Even where a reductionist explanation becomes widely accepted, it can sometimes be seen to contain its own non-rational elements. The American sociologist Robert Bellah points to the difficulties that critics of religion have run up against in their attempts to identify the hidden truth underlying the erroneous beliefs of religious people. Bellah has in mind the formulations of Freud and Durkheim and also of the German sociologist of religion Max Weber. All three were ultimately faced in their research with irreducible, non-literal concepts as central to their arguments. From the point of view of a traditional empirical scientist, there simply is nothing to get hold of in concepts like 'the unconscious' or 'effervescence', or Max Weber's central religious notion of 'charisma'. Bellah puts it as follows:[1]

> What I am suggesting is that the fact that these three great non-believers, the most seminal minds in modern social science, each in his own way ran up against non-rational, non-cognitive factors of central importance to the understanding of human action, but which did not yield readily to any available conceptual resources, is in itself a fact of great significance for religion in the twentieth century. Convinced of the invalidity of traditional religion, each rediscovered the power of the religious consciousness.

In my view, a very large proportion of scientific studies of religion and religious experience have, in the past, been severely defective in that they have approached religion from a domineering and prejudging point of view. This is to indulge in what Paul Ricoeur has called the 'hermeneutics of suspicion',[2] where because one is unable to take the realm of the sacred at face value, one must think of it as illusion or the lies of consciousness.

The alternative for Ricoeur is the 'hermeneutic of faith'. All religious behaviour, without exception, aims to interpret and act upon an experience of the sacred taken at face value. There is no reason whatsoever why social scientists cannot make a study of the world as it is experienced by a religious believer, to take that experience at face value, and to relate it to any other given aspect of the human condition that interests them.

It is primarily a matter of what scientists think they are doing when they enter into a dialogue with a religious person. There are various ways of doing this, some of them closely akin to the methods used in the physical sciences. I can study other human beings by observing them, judging them, and categorizing them, so that they become objects, subject to discoverable laws. Thus, if I were convinced by Freud's view that religious ritual is simply a manifestation of obsessional neurosis, I might decide to sit in a church for a number of days, measuring the frequency of ritual behaviour by individuals who entered the church, correlating it with things like age, sex, time of day, etc. and publish a paper called 'The demographic and social characteristics of obsessional neurosis manifested in an English parish church'. The trouble with this kind of approach is that although I may think I am being highly objective, in fact I am cutting myself off from my 'subjects', not even talking to them about what they believe they are doing. This means that the way is wide open for every kind of prejudice on my part to have free rein.

Another way I could relate to the people I observe performing their rituals in church is to arrange to have a conversation with them afterwards. I might ask them to explain to me what they were doing, while I fit their answers into a number of categories that will be useful to me when I write my academic paper. I will listen very carefully to what they have to say, attempting at the same time to interpret from my own more knowledgeable or superior standpoint what they are 'really' saying. In practice, of course, what I am doing is exercising power over them and, quite likely, remaining unaware of my own prejudgements.

Genuine conversation, on the other hand, occurs when I not only recognize the people I am talking to as fellow human beings whose limitations I share, but also their claim to be heard in their own terms. Instead of trying to 'understand' them in a dominative manner, I try to understand what they have to say, through the natural interchanges that take place in a normal conversation, as well as to learn from them. What the approach permits is the freedom to probe with some sensitivity the meaning that individuals place upon their experiences, as well as to note their social consequences.

It is extremely important to add that even when conducted in this manner, scientific research can do nothing whatever either to prove or to disprove the correctness of the religious view of life. The official stance of the Alister Hardy Research Centre is that as a research organization it can have no prior view as to the ultimate nature of religious phenomena. Whether the supernatural focus of transcendent or religious experience has reality in an absolute sense is beyond the scope of sociological investigation. Nevertheless, as I mentioned in the previous chapter, it has been possible to start questioning the assertion that religious experience is a symptom of some kind of social or individual pathology.

Religious experience and the Church

I write the above as a preface to the final pages of this book, where I want to look ahead, briefly, at one or two potential developments in the study of religious experience.

The work that I have been discussing is of scientific, medical and political, as well as religious, importance. Thus, research recently completed at the Centre, directed by Dr Geoffrey Ahern, enters into sophisticated computer-assisted ways of making a detailed classification of written accounts of religious experience. Once the method is fully developed it will enable subtle comparisons to be made between descriptions drawn from widely differing religious cultures; already plans are in hand to make a comparative study in this way of sets of accounts collected in India. The potential for improving understanding between groups split apart by political differences that have a religious root seems to me to be very great.

Another important study being done in connection with the Centre is on the relationship between transcendent experience and psychosis. Mr Michael Jackson is investigating a curious paradox. People reporting religious experience are on the whole better balanced mentally, happier, and more socially responsible than others. Yet in other circumstances, as I mentioned in an earlier chapter, experiences such as they describe can be used as evidence for the diagnosis of mental illness. The disentangling of this very complex field could lead to a revision of the way in which an illness like schizophrenia is understood.

Both of the above pieces of research deserve a presentation of book length from their respective authors, and I hope very much that this will come to pass. I want now to speak personally, from a religiously committed point of view, about three other potential directions for research in this field that I think will be of value to the churches and to religious people in general. Since I am myself a practising member of a Christian denomination, I can speak most naturally from this perspective, though I will also have very clearly in mind the idea of 'religious awareness' as something universal to the human species, and manifested in every religious culture.

The spirituality of people outside the religious institutions

A relatively small proportion of people reporting religious experience are regular church attenders. Not far short of half of those reporting experience say they *never* go to church except, perhaps, for a wedding or a funeral, yet they often say that their experience is of the highest importance to them; several would claim that it has radically changed the direction of their lives.

The reason for the disjunction between private religiousness and adherence to the religious institution is not at all clear, although of course there are plenty of guesses about it. The lack of knowledge directly affects the task of those concerned with effective mission, because as yet there is no systematic information whatever about the spiritual life of those outside the churches as distinct from those within them. Putting it in Christian terms, if it is the case that the Holy Spirit is not remote from any human being, one could ask the question, how does the Spirit communicate himself to people immersed in contemporary, secular, Britain?

Even if all the British people who claim they have had some kind of religious experience are mistaken, and I for one do not seriously believe that to be the case, it means that there is an immense group—literally tens of millions of people—remote from the churches in the sense of not belonging to them formally, yet remarkably close in terms of their inner longing and their interpretation of their experience. If the Holy Spirit does speak to every one of us, I do not see how one can easily dismiss the spirituality of this group of people.

It would be a relatively simple matter to identify a large sample of people who are outside the churches but who nevertheless report religious experience, and to examine the structure of the sample (for example its distribution according to sex, age, education, job, social class, geographical region, etc.). One could then find out about the nature of people's experience and how they interpret it; what their feelings are about formal religious groupings; what relationship they feel there is between their experience and the way religion is presented to them by the churches. Such an approach would respect the inner experience of this very large group of people and lay the basis for a constructive dialogue. The point of this is not primarily to get people sitting in pews on a Sunday, but to develop a sensitive and intelligent understanding of the nature of religion in this country, whether inside or outside the churches.

The role of religious experience in pastoral work with the sick

The initial research programme of the Hardy Centre has uncovered a number of ways in which religious experience seems to have very down-to-earth practical implications for the health of society. I have discussed in a previous chapter the striking link there appears to be with ethical behaviour. I believe there is also a very direct link with the pastoral role of the churches, particularly in the care of people who are very seriously ill. This is something I have discussed in depth with Dr David Aldridge, formerly of St Mary's Hospital, London, and the rest of this section owes much to him.

In recent years there has been a growing dissatisfaction with the ability of orthodox medicine to meet important health-care needs; hence the great increase of interest in alternative medicine, holistic living, etc. The difficulties are particularly acute in relation to the chronically sick and the terminally ill, who are faced by a series of uniquely severe personal crises in their lives. Such patients have to face the following traumas: first hearing from a doctor that they have been diagnosed as severely ill; being told that they are dying; undergoing medical examinations to make a judgement of the progress of the illness; receiving a report of the results of the examination, whether favourable or unfavourable; having to give up their employment; perhaps entering a hospice shortly before death.

Coping with this sequence of events involves patients in facing, sometimes for the first time, the need to make sense of their lives so far and to find meaning in their suffering and dying. The same is vividly true when considering the total group of people in the environment of the patient. The process of interpreting chronic sickness or terminal illness goes on not only in patients, but also in those who care for them, and influences the further search for meaning, causation and, perhaps, healing.

Increasingly, there is a demand within medicine for a recognition of the subjective experience of the individual and, because of a growing appreciation of the influence of the mind on the body, a realization of the need to understand the personal meanings of patients and those who care for them, and how these meanings affect the quality of life. A factor that appears to play a central role in the quality of life of many desperately ill patients is spiritual or religious meaning, often mediated by some kind of numinous or mystical experience, as defined earlier in this book.

At a formal level, there has been a recognition of this in the growth of the hospice movement. Informally, the same issue has been commented on in private for some years by a number of very senior members of the medical profession. It is here that the research data reported in this book become important. 'Critical junctures' are an important consideration when it is remembered how frequently religious experience is reported in association with personal crisis. This certainly applies not only to patients, but also to the nurses who care for them. In a piece of research conducted for the Alister Hardy Research Centre in 1987, Dr David Lewis found that 66 per cent of a random sample of nurses in two large hospitals reported that they had had some kind of religious experience, often in association with the care of severely ill or dying patients.

In the great majority of cases where informants make a connection between their religious or transcendent experience and their personal circumstances, the experience is seen as enabling the individual (whether patient or carer) to make an emotional adjustment to the traumatic situation; or at times it is even seen as contributing to healing of the patient.

No systematic research information is currently available on the nature or function of the spiritual experience of patients in this category; almost none exists about the experience of members of the caring community for which the patient forms the focus. A practical research programme could be mounted that would prepare, publish and disseminate a set of guidelines on the role of religious experience in the management of illness for those professionally concerned, such as doctors, nurses, social workers and clergy who have responsibility for the care of chronically sick or terminally ill people.[3]

Implications for education

Through the course of this book I have regularly returned to questions of education. I contended in the previous chapter that, in a sense, young people have been cut adrift from a genuine part of their personal experience because of a false understanding of the nature and limitations of the scientific method. Underneath the endemic suspicion within our culture, there seems to lie a very large area of religious awareness, suppressed or even repressed because of the censorship of surrounding society. For this reason, I have proposed two major tasks for those involved in religious education, both of which have the purpose of giving children access to the inner world of the religious believer in a way that is both educationally responsible and effective.[4]

1 Children in our culture need to be taught how to be aware of their own inner experience and their potential to be aware. It is only when we discover that we have such a thing as inner experience that

we are able to respect it in other people. Our society is highly extravert, demanding our attention with such a battery of continuous sensory stimulation that it more or less 'invades' and invalidates our awareness of ourselves as people who have an inner life.

Because we have investigated this question in a research project in Nottingham University, we know that the great majority of school pupils, at both primary and secondary level, are very out of touch with their own inner experience. Few young people have any experience whatever of formal methods of becoming aware, such as observing one's breathing, stilling oneself, attending to the here-and-now of experience, noticing the meanderings of the imagination. Such areas of human experience are common to everybody and are not themselves religious, but because of the narrowing of our awareness by the pressure of secular culture, they tend to be ignored. Among devout religious people, these are crucially important realms for examination, and the skills for doing so have been developed to very high levels of sophistication in the spirituality of the great world religions.

Therefore, if pupils are to gain insight into the inner nature of religion, awareness of our inner experience needs to be given formal attention in the classroom.

2 Children need to develop an understanding of the role of language and metaphor in focusing and interpreting our experience of life. In their practical activities, religious people always have an intention; for example, when they settle down to meditation or silent prayer, they do not simply enter the area of silence. They do so with an intentionality that arises from the expectations related to their culture. In Christian prayer, entering silence carries with it intentions indicated by instructions like 'wait', 'listen', 'place yourself in the presence of God'.

This is equally true of all secular activities; we never act in any circumstance, secular or religious, without some kind of intention. In the same way, Buddhist meditation has its own intentionality, just like Christian prayer, a fact not always appreciated by Western educators. Thus, the 1982 supplement of the *Birmingham Handbook on Religious Education* recommends the practice of Buddhist meditation for pupils studying comparative religion, while not at the same time advocating (for example) Christian prayer. In a way, I applaud the former, yet the implication of the omission of the latter is that Buddhist meditation is somehow religiously 'neutral'. Perhaps the apparent a-theism of Buddhism gives it the appearance of being consonant with Western secularism; yet it, like Christianity, is rooted in a total cultural complex of metaphorically mediated religious experience. The boundary line is a very difficult one to draw.

The implication of what I have said is that religious education (RE), if it is to achieve the objective of bringing about an educated understanding of the religious perspective, cannot be conducted at arm's length. Because it involves pupils' understanding of themselves, it also means that religious education needs to take seriously the currently expanding area of personal and social education (PSE). The two areas of the curriculum have been edging closer together for some time, and during the course of the developing relationship the vexed question of indoctrination has raised its head yet again.

A few years ago, in its report on *Personal and Social Education in Secondary Schools* (1983), the Schools Council Working Party on PSE included a supplementary paper by Charles Bailey on 'Spiritual and moral development'. Bailey noted, in agreement with the argument presented here, that RE that confines itself to external description of religion, fails to get at the heart of it. But he feared that the alternative is a neo-confessionalist attempt at the spiritual development of children:

> I am not a religious educator, but it does seem to me that there is
> not much point in talking about the spiritual development of
> children, if this is to have a specifically religious connotation, unless
> the advocates of bringing about such a development are clear as to
> whether the intention is to develop knowledge and understanding of
> religion within the normal bounds of rational cognitive develop-
> ment, as most teachers understand it, or to develop spiritual
> experience and insight or awareness. . . . The techniques for one
> are not, presumably, those for the other. The criteria of success for
> the former are not those for the latter; and most importantly, the
> justification for deliberately seeking to 'provoke spiritual insight', in
> social contexts where at least some people do not recognise this as
> meaningful in its religious sense [is not clear].

Presumably there is no problem about this in an overtly Christian school, where the parents intend that their children should have a grounding in their religion. But what of the religiously neutral state school?

We know that even in as secular a nation as Britain, spontaneous religious experience is very common. It is well-nigh a certainty that in every class above the third form in secondary schools (and, as I have indicated, often very much earlier) there will be some pupils who know from their own experience what the RE teacher is talking about. Some of these may formally belong to a religious group. Other members of the class, because of their upbringing, may accept intellectually the beliefs of their own religious community, but lack any confirmation from their experience. Yet others may lack both religious belief and any experience that might make them dubious of their secularism.

As I see it, the role of the RE teacher is to liberate all these sub-groups from the taboos that inhibit them from exploring freely the experiential and cognitive options available. I have indicated my view that the most massive taboo is that set up by secular metaphor, and hence this is what the teacher needs to explore most carefully. Precisely because of the strength of the social interdiction, I nevertheless think it inappropriate to conduct a direct, public investigation of the religious experience of members of the class. In the current situation this would undoubtedly do violence to the privacy of the individual. The objective is to give permission for, rather than to disclose, personal experience.

The force of my argument up to this point is that the work of the RE teacher, properly understood, is the reverse of indoctrination as feared by Bailey. The problem for most RE teachers is not the anxiety that in some way they will be indoctrinating their pupils into rigidly religious ways of thinking, but that the minds of the pupils are tightly closed against the possibility that reality might plausibly be seen in any other way than that transmitted via the dominant culture. Religious education undertaken from a genuinely open perspective attempts to assist pupils to set aside temporarily their presuppositions, when trying to understand how someone with different beliefs from their own perceives the world. By developing awareness of their own inner experience, and an understanding of the power of metaphor and symbol to structure our perspective on reality, pupils become more able to empathize and sympathize with those whose perspective differs from their own.

The teacher is not attempting to convert pupils to any particular belief, but to increase their insight into other ways of seeing. It is quite true that a pupil might come to choose one of the perspectives presented, but that is a free choice, and in no sense the result of indoctrination. What makes religious education have supreme signi-ficance in the educational system, well beyond the bounds of its own discipline, is its role in broadening understanding within a deeply divided multi-faith and multi-ethnic society. In other words, one of its primary functions is de-indoctrination.

Conclusion

I end as I began, with Manchester College, Estlin Carpenter and Alister Hardy. It seems to me as a Roman Catholic, and therefore an outsider to Unitarianism, that its special genius is its ability to foster a self-confident relaxation on the boundary where science and religion meet. It was said of Estlin Carpenter that 'of even temporary doubt or unbelief he had no experience whatever'. The same might have been said of many a late Victorian, brought up within the sheltered environment of parsonage or manse. But Carpenter was not sheltered thus. He was the son of an eminent physiologist, saw science as 'one of the various influences that have been at work in educating our religious conception', and held strongly to an evolutionary view both in biology and in his understanding of the origins of religion.

He thus understood our religious nature as something profoundly built into us as biological organisms. If we use our reasoning powers to ponder honestly upon the total experience of being human, we cannot avoid taking this into account. Failure to do so means that we arrive at a crippled understanding of our species. Carpenter was more than willing to reason, but he knew that 'reasoning cannot bring God into the conclusion if he is not first found in the premises', and these arose from an even deeper intuition than we have of the physical universe around us: 'I see that the world contains not the infinity we feel; rather does this infinity contain the world'.

When Hardy set up the Religious Experience Research Unit in Manchester College, more than 50 years after Carpenter had retired as principal, he brought something of the same passionate conviction to his efforts. His utter certainty of the reality of his own religious experience enabled him to sustain a boyhood vow that most people would have forgotten in the excitement of a highly successful scientific career.

Hardy's professional scientific work was as value-free as the next person's, but so-called value-free research is carried out, in all cases and without exception, by human beings who do have values. He never concealed his personal beliefs, which I am sure damaged his efforts to obtain funding for his research in the field of religion.

I was in attendance once when representatives of a very important funding agency were considering an application from the Unit. At one point Hardy tried to emphasize the importance of the project in a way that he must have often used in successful applications for support for biological research. All research scientists often use this kind of rhetoric. 'I just *know* there is something there', he said, slapping the table with his hand. I groaned inwardly, because I knew that in that moment he had lost the opportunity of a grant. It was two or three hundred years since European culture had decided to split the seamless robe of human experience, and religious experience fell on the wrong side of the divide.

Hardy believed the torn garment could be mended by a broader, more human view of science:

Those who are concerned lest our civilisation will change its nature under the influence of a materialistic philosophy might, I believe, do well to consider how they might encourage further research into the nature of human personality, in the hope of finding more about the nature of God. The great institutes for scientific research have a bearing on man's bodily comfort—upon medical problems direct and indirect, agriculture and fisheries, food, transport and so on—are dotted about the country, and are as symbolic of the present age as our glorious cathedrals and parish churches are symbolic of our spiritual past. If only one per cent of the money spent upon the physical and biological sciences could be spent . . . it might not be long before a new age of faith dawned upon the world. It would, I believe, be a faith in a spiritual reality to match that of the middle ages; one based not upon a belief in a miraculous interference with the course of nature, but upon a greatly widened scientific outlook. What might mankind not do if he used the tools of modern science with the faith and inspiration of the cathedral builders? Can the scientific method help to re-establish such a faith? Let us have the faith to try.

As a Christian, committed to a theology of Grace, I believe there is a further dimension to take into account. Nevertheless, I cannot but heartily concur with the need for science and scientists to take a much wider view of their field of activity. My confident hope would then be identical with that of Alister Hardy.

Notes

1   R. N. Bellah, *Beyond Belief* (New York: Harper & Row, 1970).

2   Paul Ricoeur, *Freud and Philosophy: An Essay in Interpretation* (Yale University Press, 1970).

3   A piece of research on this theme is currently being conducted by Belinda Huddleson in the sociology department of Exeter University, under the direction of Dr Grace Davie and with the assistance of the Alister Hardy Research Centre.

4   David Hay, 'Suspicion of the spiritual: teaching R.E. in a world of secular experience', *British Journal of Religious Education*, vol. 7 (1985), p. 140. See also J. Hammond *et al.*, *New Methods in R.E. Teaching: An Experiential Approach* (London: Oliver & Boyd/Longman, 1990).

Bibliography

American Psychiatric Association (1987) *Diagnostic and Statistical Manual of Mental Disorders: DSM-3-R*, 3rd edn—revised: (Washington: American Psychiatric Association)

Back, K and Bourque, L. B. (1970) 'Can feelings be enumerated?', *Behavioral Science*, vol. 15, p. 487

Beardsworth, T. (1977) *A Sense of Presence* (Oxford: Religious Experience Research Unit, Manchester College)

Bellah, R. N. (1970) *Beyond Belief* (New York: Harper & Row)

Berger, P. (1979) *Facing Up to Modernity* (Harmondsworth: Penguin Books)

Carpenter, J. E. (1913) *Comparative Religion* (London: Home University Library)

Comte, A. (1965) *Cours de Philosophie Positive*, quoted by E. E. Evans-Pritchard in *Theories of Primitive Religion* (Oxford: Clarendon Press)

Draper, J. W. (1874) *A History of the Warfare Between Science and Religion* (New York)

Durkheim, E. (1915) *The Elementary Forms of the Religious Life*, trans. J. W. Swain (London: Allen & Unwin)

Edwards, J. (1746) *A Treatise Concerning the Religious Affections* (republished Edinburgh: Banner of Truth Trust, 1986)

Erb, P. C. (ed.) (1983) *Pietists: Selected Writings* (London: SPCK)

Fowler, J. (1981) *Stages of Faith* (San Francisco: Harper & Row)

Gallup Poll (1978) *Religion in America: The Gallup Opinion Index 1977–78* (Princeton: AIPO)

Gallup Poll (1985a) '4 in 10 Americans have had unusual spiritual experiences' (Princeton: AIPO press release)

Gallup Poll (with AHRC) (1985b) Unpublished national poll of reports of religious experience in Britain

Godin, A. (1985) *Psychological Dynamics of Religious Experience* (Birmingham, Alabama: Religious Education Press)

Goldman, R. (1964) *Religious Thinking from Childhood to Adolescence* (London: Routledge & Kegan Paul)

Greeley, A. M. (1975) *The Sociology of the Paranormal: A Reconnaissance* (Sage Research Papers in the Social Sciences, Studies in Religion and Ethnicity Series no. 90–023; Beverly Hills and London: Sage Publications)

Hall, G.S. (1904) *The Psychology of Adolescence* (2 vols; New York and London: D. Appleton & Co.)

Hammond, J., Hay, D., Moxon, J., Netto, B., Raban, K., Straugheir, G., and Williams, C. (1990) *New Methods in R.E. Teaching: An Experiential Approach* (London: Oliver & Boyd/Longman)

Happold, F.C. (1970) *Mysticism: A Study and an Anthology* (Harmondsworth: Penguin Books)

Hardy, A.C. (1948) *The Faith of a Scientist* (London: Lindsey Press)

Hardy, A.C. (1951) 'Science and the Quest for God', *Essex Hall Lecture* (London: Lindsey Press)

Hardy, A.C. (1966) *The Divine Flame: An Essay Towards a Natural History of Religion* (London: Collins)

Hardy, A.C. (1979) *The Spiritual Nature of Man* (Oxford: Clarendon Press)

Hardy, A.C. (1984) *Darwin and the Spirit of Man* (London: Collins)

Hardy, A.C. (n.d.) Autobiography (unpublished)

Hay, D. (1979) 'Religious experience amongst a group of post-graduate students: a qualitative study', *Journal for the Scientific Study of Religion*, vol. 18(2), p. 164

Hay, D. (1985) 'Suspicion of the spiritual: teaching R.E. in a world of secular experience', *British Journal of Religious Education*, vol. 7, p. 140

Hay, D. (1987) *Exploring Inner Space*, 2nd edn (Oxford: Mowbray)

Hay, D. and Heald, G. (1987) 'Religion is good for you', *New Society* (17 April)

Hay, D. and Morisy, A. (1978) 'Reports of ecstatic, paranormal or religious experience in Britain and the United States: a comparison of trends', *Journal for the Scientific Study of Religion*, vol. 17(3), p. 255

Hay, D. and Morisy, A. (1985) 'Secular society/religious meanings: a contemporary paradox', *Review of Religious Research*, vol. 26(3), p. 213

Herford, C.H. (ed.) (1929) *Joseph Estlin Carpenter: A Memorial Volume* (Oxford: Clarendon Press)

James, W. (1902) *The Varieties of Religious Experience: A Study in Human Nature* (London: Fontana, 1960; New York: Penguin American Library, 1982)

Jefferies, R. (1949) *The Story of My Heart* (London: Eyre & Spottiswoode)

Johnston, W. (1976) *Silent Music* (London: Fontana)

Jung, C.G. (1973) *Synchronicity: An A-Causal Connecting Principle* (Bollingen Series; Princeton University Press)

Laski, M. (1961) *Ecstasy: A Study of Some Secular and Religious Experiences* (London: Cresset Press)

Leuba, J. (1925) *The Psychology of Religious Mysticism* (London: Kegan Paul, Trench, Trubner & Co.)

McLellan, D. (1987) *Marxism and Religion* (London: Macmillan)

Maringer, J. (1960) *The Gods of Prehistoric Man* (London: Weidenfeld & Nicolson)

Martin, B. and Pluck, R. (1977) *Young People's Beliefs* (Church of England Board of Education)

Marx, K. and Engels, F. (1972) *On Religion* (Moscow: Progress Publishers)

Maxwell, M. and Tschudin, V. (1990) *Seeing the Invisible: Modern Religious and Other Transcendent Experiences* (Harmondsworth: Penguin Books)

Meissner, W.W., SJ, MD (1984) *Psychoanalysis and Religious Experience* (New Haven, Connecticut: Yale University Press)

Milgram, S. (1974) *Obedience and Authority* (London: Tavistock Press)

Morgan Research (1983) Unpublished national poll of reports of religious experience in Australia

Newman, J.H. (1864) *Apologia pro Vita Sua* (republished London: Fontana, 1959)

Otto, R. (1950) *The Idea of the Holy*, trans. J.W. Harvey (Oxford University Press)

Paley, W. (1802) *Natural Theology; or, Evidences of the Existence and Attributes of the Deity collected from the Appearances of Nature* (London)

Persinger, M.A. (1983) 'Religious and mystical experiences as artefacts of temporal lobe function: a general hypothesis', *Perceptual and Motor Skills*, vol. 57, p. 1255

Popper, K. (1959) *The Logic of Scientific Discovery* (London: Hutchinson)

Pourrat, P. (1930) *Christian Spirituality*, trans. S.P. Jaques (3 vols; London: Burns Oates & Washbourne)

Princeton Religion Research Center (PRRC) (1978) *The Unchurched American* (PRRC/AIPO)

Ricoeur, P. (1970) *Freud and Philosophy: An Essay in Interpretation* (Yale University Press)

Robinson, E. (1983) *The Original Vision* (New York: Seabury Press)

Robinson, E. and Jackson, M. (1987) *Religion and Values at 16 +* (Alister Hardy Research Centre and the Christian Education Movement)

Starbuck, E.D. (1899) *The Psychology of Religion: An Empirical Study of the Growth of Religious Consciousness* (New York: Walter Scott)

Tanquerey, A. (1930) *The Spiritual Life* (New York: Desclee & Co.)

Towler, R. (1974) *Homo Religiosus* (London: Constable)

West, M. (1979) 'Meditation', *British Journal of Psychiatry*, vol. 135, p. 457

Wuthnow, R. (1976) *Peak Experiences: Some Empirical Tests* (Berkeley: University of California, Survey Research Center)